Seven

In the Lane of Hope

Michael J. Marini

Scriptures taken from the Holy Bible, New International Version®, NIV®. Copyright © 1973, 1978, 1984, 2011 by Biblica, Inc.™ Used by permission of Zondervan. All rights reserved worldwide. www.zondervan.com.

The "NIV" and "New International Version" are trademarks registered in the United States Patent and Trademark Office by Biblica, Inc.

Copyright © 2018 Michael J. Marini

All rights reserved.

ISBN: 172574192X
ISBN-13: 978-1725741928

To our Father, who truly has it all in His hands – us included.

"To give anything less than your best is to sacrifice the gift."
— **Steve Prefontaine**
racing legend of the 1970s

CONTENTS

Foreword – Not Your Average Story i

Genesis – The Starting Line 1

Prologue – The Night Before Christmas 5

Chapter 1 – First Thing This Morning 7

Chapter 2 – The First Lap 19

Chapter 3 – Lap Number Two 34

Chapter 4 – Patricia: The Boss 42

Chapter 5 – Denise: The Champ 52

Chapter 6 – Linda: The Rock 73

Chapter 7 – Kathleen: The Heart of Seven 84

Chapter 8 – Marianne: The Dream Painter 94

Chapter 9 – Theresa: The Blooming Flower 126

Chapter 10 – Angela: The Little Angel 144

Chapter 11 – Lap Three 155

Chapter 12 – Hitting Light on the Bell Lap 173

Chapter 13 – In the Lane of Hope 179

Revelation – The Finish Line 186

Thoughts From the Heart 189

Pop's Quotes Through the Years 195

FOREWORD
Not Your Average Story

When was the last time you heard an actually uplifting story that was true? Something that made you go, "Wow! There is still hope for humankind!"

These days, those kinds of real-life accounts can seem a little hard to find, particularly in our various media outlets – and that includes social media. When we turn on the news, we're bound to get much more of the bad kind than anything good – wars and famines and riots, and far too many other signs of people hurting people.

Once those tragic tales have been reported from every angle possible, next up is the political updates, which boil down to mere political agendas more often than not: opinions being snipped and snapped at viewers, and rammed down our already sore throats. The same applies to the technological advancements that, we're told, were made to bring us together. Our so-called "social" media platforms are about as social as the Civil War was civil.

It's almost enough to give up on the future altogether.

But should it be? Are those outlets (or inlets) truly a reflection of our world? And even if they are, are we helplessly destined to be buried beneath it all? Have we pushed selfishness and division and sorrow so far that we've trapped ourselves inside the tormented pages of Dante's *Inferno*, complete with a fiery Hell we can't escape? *Seven* says not so fast.

We're not there yet, it assures. In fact, there are signs of the very opposite all around us, little bits of Heaven on Earth to light our way through to eternity.

This is not a story that denies reality. Instead, it's one that sees reality from a much wider perspective: an overarching viewpoint that already knows – for a fact – that the freeing, uplifting, game-changing truth will cross that finish line... while its opposition is left lying in the dust.

A story of hope that acknowledges the negative – the hurtful and disappointing and confusing – but rises above it, the following pages track a family of 13 through life's ups and downs to a striking conclusion you don't want to miss.

I dare you not to be encouraged by the end.

– Jeannette DiLouie
author of the Founding America series

GENESIS
The Starting Line

It's not like I don't know the holiday season is the most stressful time of year for most people. They say that drinking and bar visits and suicides go up around that time – although I've also heard that last statistic is completely made up.

Who knows. But let's face it, Christmastime can be involved, to say the least. There's the present-buying. There's the "making sure you made your list and checked it twice" – or perhaps 15 times over, obsessively asking yourself if you missed someone like you did last year.

There's the money spent, knowing full well you'll have to deal with your credit card in a month. And there's the lack of sunlight that seems to sap energy every extra step of the way as we buy groceries and make food and decorate and try to keep everyone as happy as possible.

Again, I understand the holidays are a difficult time for many people; emotions run deeper, loved ones are missed more, and everything is intensified. For my part, I've certainly struggled with the run-up to it, especially with my family business being what it is. Things get utterly chaotic and exhausting during that time – more so than mere words can express.

Honestly, most Decembers are little more than a blur to me, with my parents and 10 siblings and assorted other family members losing sleep – so much sleep! – making and decorating Christmas wreaths, collecting and glittering pinecones, lighting and adorning hundreds of miniature trees, and selling a couple thousand bigger ones while trying to keep the shop clean and customers satisfied.

To call it a full-time job doesn't do it justice. I have a hunch even Santa Claus would be impressed with what my family manages to accomplish each year. And each year, we seem to come together to get the job done by December 25, when we can all finally rejoice in the end of another season, sit down and enjoy the fruits of our labor.

The Christmas of 2011 was one notable exception. That was the year I lost my sense of joy and hope and ever-present (or at least typically-present) love. That was the year I thought I was going to lose everything that made Christmas truly Christmas.

That was the year my family's foundation was tested and we got our true wake-up call.

But before I tell you about that, there's something you need to know...

In the Beginning

Many years ago, I had a very unique dream that's since stuck with me through the years. If you're skeptical about its details, I don't blame you at all. But it did happen. And it touched me so vividly, both in the moment and down the road. So I can't help but believe it was something more than my subconscious at work.

In the fated dream, an angel came to me and handed me a book. It had an ornate gold cover with a white script that read, "Seven." It was glowing as I held it, and I could faintly hear the sound of a piano playing in the distance. Before I could open it though, the angel took my hand and told me to follow her. That was when I recognized I was in my old childhood bedroom and as we stepped out of it, we walked together down the hallway toward the kitchen. There, my seven sisters were all sitting at their usual seats around our well-worn table.

"My sisters are here!" I exclaimed, pointing first to my oldest sister, Patti.

THE STARTING LINE

"Her name is Hope," my guide responded.

"No, that's Patti," I objected, then looked around, confused. "Is someone playing piano in the other room?"

But she didn't answer, too focused on identifying my sisters. As I looked around, my eyes next fell on my sisters Denise and Linda, and the angel told me I was looking at Patience and Peace. Kate, my middle sister, was recognized as Grace. And Marianne, Theresa and Angela were called Faith, Love and Joy, respectively.

Then the angel told me that the book I held in my hand and the story I saw in front of me were one and the same. When I asked her what I was supposed to do with this information, she told me, "Keep it safe for now and at the right time, it will be opened."

With that, she took the book back and placed seven stars in my right hand even as the piano music swelled around me. "The light of the stars and the music in your spirit will guide you, Michael. Listen to the song in your heart. The words you write will come through the music."

I can still remember those words so well, just as I remember her taking my hand and leading me back to my room. She told me to rest now because it would be a long journey to complete the book.

This brought up a very important question as she turned to leave.

"I'm not a writer," I protested. "I can't write a book! I was a B student in English. At best!"

In my mind, she clearly had the wrong person.

Yet the angel told me that everything would be alright and that the spirit of my sisters would lead me. As she tucked me back into bed, she whispered in my ear, "The spirit of seven will guide your way."

I had so many other questions for her, but that was when my obnoxiously loud alarm clock startled me awake, showing the time at 7:07. I could hear birds chirping outside my window, and a sliver of light was creeping through the blinds...

It was time to get to work. And as I'd been taught my whole life, when there's a job to do, you get that job done.

As it turned out, there was a lot of work to get to – more than I could have ever dreamed. Putting pen to paper has been such a worthwhile journey, filled with so many revelations about life, living, God and family. All four of those have been consistent focal points in my existence thanks to my father, Dante.

An agriculturist by occupation and a God-fearing man by design, he has cultivated quite the legacy. Being who and what he is, my dad knows what he's doing when it comes to all aspects of growing. It comes as no surprise that the seeds he planted in me and each of my 10 siblings were able to develop and blossom as any well-tended field will do. In particular, I saw firsthand how my father sowed the seeds of goodness in my seven sisters and then how those gifts were reaped during an unexpected time of grave illness.

One of his favorite sayings as we grew up was, "If this isn't Heaven, it's at least in the same zip code." After fighting off an early death and rising from his bed on Christmas Day thanks to the spiritual gifts my sisters brought him, he came to a realization that maybe we're not just in the same zip code as Heaven… maybe we're actually in it.

Sometimes, wake-up calls are exactly what we need. Though, of course, they never feel that way while we're going through them. They feel like trials, something no family wants to deal with but no family can ever completely escape when called to face them. Addiction. Abuse. Loss of work. Health struggles. There are so many hardships life can carry along the way. Yet the antidote to life's tribulations can be found if we just know where to look for it: Hope.

This story reveals how my family's much-tested yet undying hope, as modeled by my father, and our love for one another has enabled us to overcome some of the hurdles and disappointments we've had to face, as any family inevitably does. It's a journey of real-life experiences that uncover the truth that we all uniquely possess our own keys to finding Heaven on Earth.

If you believe in miracles and the underdog in each of us that stands a fighting chance, you've found your book. This is a story for all ages, meant for all ages, and to be enjoyed by all ages. I truly hope it touches you as much to read it as it did for me to live it out.

PROLOGUE
The Night Before Christmas

"Michael, is that you?" My father's voice was weak. Weak, pained and full of sorrow.

"Yeah, Pop," I assured him, reaching for his hand as he lay there in the hospital bed. "It's me. I'm with you now."

He tried to swallow around the feeding tube threaded through his throat. "I don't want to die here, Michael. I still have more to do."

"I know, Pop. We'll get you out of here." I kept my tone steady despite my own thoughts and feelings at seeing him there looking that way. "Marianne, Linda and Patti are working on it as we speak."

"They're telling me this is it." His right hand twisted in the white blankets on top of him. "The odds are against me, Michael."

"It's okay. Everyone knows you can beat the odds."

But inside, I was pleading. *Please beat the odds, Pop. Please.*

"Did you hear about your sisters?"

"Yeah, I heard."

His lips turned upward fondly. "They have a way of being at

SEVEN

their best when I'm at my worst. Thank God for your mother too."

"I know." I managed a smile as well. "She was here the whole time. Didn't leave your side until I got here."

"I'm scared," he admitted. "I just don't want to die here. This is not how I want my story to end."

Despite my best efforts, I could feel tears starting to well in my eyes. Yet I pulled on our family traditions some more for his sake.

"Just remember what Nu-nu said," I urged. "*Se Dio sta scrivendo la storia, è sicuro di avere un lieto fine.*"

Translated, it means that if God is writing the story, it's sure to have a happy ending. Nu-nu also liked to say, "*Proprio come un musicista, ama concludere con una nota alta e lo fa sempre.*" Just like a musician, He loves to end on a high note, and He always does.

Outside the hospital window, the city's Christmas lights were glowing in the distance, and a full moon had lit up the sky. Even then, I knew there were millions of children nestled snug in their beds, dreaming of the presents that awaited them, staring up at that singular moon, hoping for Santa to bring them their wish list of toys.

My dream, of course, was for a miracle for my pop.

As if on cue, when I turned back to him, he smiled and closed his eyes then fell right back to sleep.

I pulled up a chair and sat down...

CHAPTER 1
First Thing This Morning

You're right where you need to be.

It was one of the worst of times for my family. On December 25, 2011, we were in unprecedented distress and all hands were on deck for our sinking ship. According to the doctors, my father was on his deathbed even though he hadn't yet stopped fighting for his life.

When I woke up that Christmas morning, the clock read 6:37 a.m., which meant I hadn't gotten nearly enough rest. As I looked out the third-floor hospital window into the day breaking before me, I could see the sunrise just peeking in the distance. My neck was stiff and my back was sore from sleeping in the rock-hard hospital chair, but I knew those aches were nothing compared to what my father would be feeling when he woke up.

This would be his third day in the hospital, relegated to his bed, attached to tubes and feeling trapped in the unnatural position of being almost completely dependent on others. Best-case scenario, he wouldn't be allowed to walk, work or go home for many more days.

Worst-case scenario, he would never go home again.

SEVEN

Farmer Hours

Pop had been rushed to the hospital on December 22. It was right as we were starting to wrap up the 49th year of our family Christmas business, selling countless trees, along with wreaths and other homemade holiday items to people near and far. Most years, it seemed we inevitably helped our customers get into the spirit just as we were wishing Christmas would be over already.

The business was well-known in our tiny corner of Delaware, the Small Wonder State. So the work was hard, and the days were long. Even at 77, my father was still the first one out the door each morning and the last one to come in at night. Most days, he worked from 7:00 in the morning until 9:00 in the evening.

You could say it was hardly a relaxing itinerary.

"Farmer hours" is what he called his work schedule. He was the backbone of the business, and he knew it. So he never let up. He never rested the way he should have. While we told him to slow down every single Christmas season, this was the year that would actually force him to listen.

Loaded Wagons

I suppose that habits are too easily formed because, outside of our routine warnings to take care of himself (ones we knew he wouldn't heed), none of us really paid attention to the fact that he was working outside in brutal conditions all day, every day for over a month. We especially didn't notice when each Christmas season seemed busier than the last.

My father didn't believe in taking days off, so his body never had time to recover from the brutal workload the business automatically brings with it. He used to recite, "Even though the horse is blind, just load the wagon," when there was any bickering about getting a job done. It was a reminder to just do the work and not worry about anything else but the job at hand.

As such, looking back, what happened should not have been surprising. Yet it did come as a shock at the time.

On December 21, he began to look extremely pale and started running a fever. In the spirit of self-preservation, he ended his workday a whole four hours early, declaring "This is like a day off to me!" Unfortunately, a few extra hours of rest couldn't undo weeks' worth of overworking and it finally caught up with him the following morning.

At first, he was unable to get out of bed. Then he became unresponsive altogether.

Of course, my mom dialed 911. Then she notified Patti, my oldest sister, and the news flowed right on down the line from there.

Patti called Denise.
Denise called Linda.
Linda called Kate.
Kate called Marianne.
Marianne called Theresa.
Theresa called my youngest sister, Angela.

After Angela found out, she contacted my three brothers and me. This telephone chain occurred in fewer than five minutes, a testament to my family's efficiency.

Upon his arrival at the hospital, tests were immediately done and diagnoses quickly followed. It appeared he was suffering from pancreatitis and the prognosis for survival, let alone a quick recovery, was questionable at best.

Sitting alone with him three days later, I saw him move his head and start to wake up. His usually robust voice was quiet, almost inaudible, a fact my brain had trouble processing.

There he was, the strong patriarch I knew and loved, just without any of the energy he usually possessed. His face was veiled under a dark shadow, his body hidden under blankets, tubes tugging at his arms and throat…

The sight and sound of his current state was almost too foreign to bear.

Heaven-Sent

"Thank God for your mom and sisters," my father told me after he woke up again. "They always have something positive to say after the doctor drops more bad news on me. These doctors and nurses may think they're calling the shots, but I'm just going to keep listening to your mother and sisters."

He wasn't wrong to trust them when Mom and three of her daughters were all nurses. Plus, they had been right there with him in one form or another the whole time. My mother especially. The night before, she'd gone home to eat with the family and it was the first time she'd left his side since he'd been rushed to the ER in the back of an ambulance, accompanied by two of my sisters.

With pride in his voice, he asked me, "Did you hear all the things they've done since I got here? They've taken over this hospital."

I could see a small smile, and his eyes lit up a bit as he thought about them further. With good reason, too. I could easily imagine them moving into the room with determination, assessing the situation and, yes, taking over just as they had a tendency of doing.

Qualifications for Sainthood

As I tucked the blankets around him, I assured him I had indeed received their reports on the situation. That got another small smile out of him.

"We sure do have a great team in our family." There was that pride again. "Your mother is a heck of a coach. I'm not sure who we'd have to talk to, but I think she has all the qualifications for sainthood."

That made me laugh, despite myself.

I don't think he objected to the lighthearted response, but he still made sure to look me straight in the eye with his next statement. "Your mother is the best teammate a guy could ever ask for in life. When I get out of here, I really will write a strong letter of recommendation to the pope."

I knew he was serious about that sentiment, but it did seem to call for a little good-natured mockery all the same. "Well, she did raise 11 children. And she put up with you for over half a century so maybe she has a shot."

That made him laugh too. Laugh and reminisce. By the look on his face, he appeared to be remembering every moment of their time together. He may have been 77 years old, but his eyes lit up like a kid on Christmas morning as he continued thinking about Mom. And, admittedly, with good reason.

Bernardine, or "Beebe" as she's fondly known, has been something of a resident celebrity at our family's business. Her warm embrace, welcoming smile and goodie baskets filled with small toys have greeted generations of customers passing through our garage. From opening to closing time, she can be found in her usual position behind the desk, wearing her lucky red "Marini

Christmas" sweatshirt during the holiday season, complete with her favorite blue fingerless gloves.

Her unconditional love and strength of character have been the backbone of my family's team and have seen us through all manner of good and bad times. No one knew that better than my father.

Dante's Angels

Right about then, there was a small commotion outside the hospital room that, after many years of experience, I knew could only be one thing. It marked the arrival of my sisters.

It wasn't just a few of them coming into the room either. It was all seven. They entered in a single-file line that just so happened to be in order of age. Patti led the way, followed by Denise, Linda, Kate, Marianne, Theresa, and last but not least, Angela bringing up the rear complete with an aura of beaming light and purpose.

In *Charlie's Angels*, there were three heavenly messengers. My father, however, beat him by far. He had seven. And even though it was only 9:30 on Christmas morning, they had all left their families to come visit him.

The rising sun was shining directly into the room now and it appeared to be glowing around each of my sisters. When I asked Marianne why they were all there so early, she told me, "We wanted to get here first thing this morning."

It wasn't often I got to see them together, but when all seven were present and accounted for, it was like viewing a work of art. A human masterpiece, really. At least that's how I saw it.

On the rare occasions that all 13 family members were out in public together, people would often stop and stare. Most were probably unsure of what to think when they saw us rolling into a restaurant with our baker's dozen, each person resembling the next.

When that happened, Linda would remind us, "They're just stopping to watch the freak show. Just look straight ahead and don't stare back."

Seven's Heaven

Now with all seven in the room, they settled into the situation at hand and took up their positions as if they were following a script. Linda and Patti, in particular, were both saying how lucky we were that they knew some of the staff.

"There should only be three of us in here," they explained, "but they let us sneak in a few extra."

As was customary for me when all seven of the girls were together, I stood back and got out of the way so as not to be run over. Yet this time was somehow different. This time, I saw them exactly as they were.

Returning to my original position back in the chair, I watched them crowd around our father. In front of me were seven angels sent from above at the precise time he needed them most. He needed a miracle and, sure enough, he now had seven surrounding him.

True to form, they never visited anyone empty-handed. Since we had about 15 wreaths left when the business closed down for the season, my sisters decided to bring them all to the hospital as gifts for the staff. A minute after they entered the room, Angela was already busy running around giving a wreath to each of the nurses, doctors, and front-desk staff, spreading Christmas joy wherever she went.

I'll admit I was secretly hoping those gestures would get them to take extra special care of our dad in room 313.

Final Exams

Linda, Marianne and Patti had all converged on my father's chart, studying it like three students cramming before a final exam. Their faces bore a look of intensity as they read over the chart.

Kate, who had just arrived after a seven-hour drive from upstate New York, quickly assessed the scene. "Let's push his bed a little closer to the window so he can look outside and get more natural light." She turned to me. "Michael, can you give me a hand? You get one end, and I'll get the other."

With that, I sprung out of my seat to follow her lead. Under her guidance, we moved his bed from the dark corner of the room into the light of Christmas Day.

Out of the Darkness

As usual, Denise was doing two things at once. Rearranging his cards and flowers so he could see them from his new bed position, she was simultaneously speaking on the phone with Mom, who was babysitting some of the grandkids.

Mom would be coming down later in the day after all my sisters left. It was entirely typical of her to put everyone before herself. And it was entirely typical of Denise to be giving her a minute-by-minute report as she fixed up the room.

"He looks a little better," she was saying. "Some of his color is coming back, and Kate and Michael just moved his bed out of a dark corner into a sunny spot."

A slight pause on her end, then, "Angela is dealing with the nurses so we can all be in here. And Patti, Linda and Marianne said his vital signs are getting better."

Mom must have said something like, "Good!" because there was another slight stop to Denise's rundown before she was off again. "Well, Theresa is sitting on the bed making him look handsome for you. We have it all under control."

Taking charge and comforting at the same time, she added, "I know he can't wait to see you. He keeps asking for you. But for now, he's right where he needs to be."

I wasn't even slightly surprised that this was her parting thought to Mom considering our family history.

Heart & Sole

Being that my parents had 11 children, it's no wonder we all participated in an activity that only required a pair of sneakers and nothing else but a lot of heart. We all grew up running, including my father. It was the sport that "ran" through our blood.

My father loved coaching and enjoyed cheering for us when we ran. As such, he had a plethora of special quotes at his disposal. "You're right where you need to be" topped the list. It was the kind of statement that alleviated our fears, especially during the big races when nerves were at their peak.

It's not like he said it all the time. But when he did, you knew not to worry because he was seeing something you weren't able to.

It was like hearing the calming voice of God here on Earth.

Angels Do It Best When It's Needed Most

Each of my sisters was taking care of business in her own way.

SEVEN

None of them could change the larger situation, they just did what they could, each giving her best to make our father feel relaxed and take away any fears he had. Just as he used to do for us.

The only one who wasn't doing much talking to anyone but our dad in the process was Theresa. She was scared, and it showed in her tired eyes.

Sitting on his bed, she combed his hair, whispering to him as she did. "We're all here. Everything is going to be alright now."

She put another pillow under his legs, and then repeated those famous seven words that Denise had uttered: "You're right where you need to be."

He smiled as she said it, and I could only imagine what images that line brought to his head.

After she finished sprucing him up, Theresa slowly removed a sunflower from her bag, being careful not to harm it. It hadn't bloomed yet, but she put it in a little cup with water and placed it right next to his bed.

It would be the first thing he'd see every morning when he opened his eyes and would hopefully bring some comfort and a little holiday joy.

Then she just held his hand in silence. Her eyes were closed, but I could see the tears trickling down her face as she quietly prayed. The love she had for our father was obvious to me as I watched from across the room.

She was giving every ounce of love she had in her heart. It was Theresa at her best.

Pleiades

The stars were certainly in line for my father that Christmas morning.

In both astronomy and astrology, the constellation known as the Seven Sisters is referred to as the Pleiades. It's among the nearest cluster of stars to Earth and is the easiest one to see with the naked eye. In classical mythology, the Pleiades were the seven daughters of Atlas who were placed among the stars to save them from the overzealous hunter, Orion.

I was now seeing that situation somewhat reversed in my seven sisters. My father's seven stars were sent to protect him while he fought for his life. They may not have been arranged in a noticeable pattern down here on Earth – as a matter of fact, they were all over the room – but their lights were shining bright like seven stars in the clear night's sky as they did what they had come to do: Bring gifts and brighten up the room.

After about an hour of making sure everything was in place, Patti declared in a matter-of-fact voice, "Well, our work here is done! Is everyone ready to go?"

With that, each of them gathered their pocketbooks, bags and coats, and exited the same way they'd entered – as if they were on a heavenly mission. And as they did, I saw exactly what my dad had been talking about the previous night.

The seven sister stars had intentionally left their brilliance behind. They'd had a profound effect on him, and I could feel his newfound hope and relief as I held his hand.

Some of the Best Medicine

Sitting in that room, I have to say, it was one of those times in life I felt lucky to be single. Right then, my only responsibility was to be with my father, and that was exactly where I needed to be.

Before Marianne had left the room, she'd whispered to me, "Just stay with him until Mom gets here. Keep his spirits high and stay positive."

Linda's parting words had been delivered at a more normal volume. "Keep feeding him Rocky quotes. That's the best medicine for him right now."

My sisters were still laughing at that latter set of instructions as they walked down the hallway away from the room and toward the elevators. It felt like the party was leaving the building in the same manner a musician exits the stage after the final encore and the lights come on.

I could hear the elevator open and all of them stepping inside amidst a flurry of loud amusement. Then the door closed on them, ushering in the perfect silence to highlight the perfect message.

The party had indeed left the building, but its effects remained.

As Pop put it, "You couldn't write it any better if you tried."

Gonna Fly Now

As it turned out, the USA network was playing a Christmas Day

Rocky marathon, which I knew Pop would love. Linda was right. It was better than any of the three different kinds of medicine he was being given every four hours.

Even though the television was muted, we both knew those movies so well that we didn't need to hear them. The *Rocky* series was one of the most-watched film collections in my house growing up. So, naturally, my father and I knew every line.

After a bit, he started looking tired and told me he was ready for another nap. Or, as he put it, "rest my eyes for a few minutes."

He slowly closed his eyes, and as the "non-Rocky" type of medicine took effect, I decided to follow Theresa's lead. While he slept, I held his hand and sent prayers up to the heavens, hoping that an angel would hear me. Considering the visit some had already made, I thought my chances were pretty good that others were nearby and listening.

Love Is Hope… It Fuels Our Dreams

My father woke up many hours later to the commotion of a doctor and two nurses as they entered the room. He'd been asleep so long that *Rocky IV* was now playing in the background.

This latest check-in, like so many of the others before it, didn't come with good news. The odds, they said, were against him. So was his age. His body was failing, and they were giving him a 50% chance of making it through surgery.

Still bolstered by my sisters and *Rocky*, my dad tuned out the medical odds being directed at him. No longer emotionally frail, he quite simply didn't feel it was his time yet. And, as far as he was concerned, it wasn't.

The whole time the doctor and nurses spoke, his eyes stayed riveted on what was happening on the TV screen. It was the first training montage of the movie, with Rocky running up the mountains somewhere in Siberia.

It actually made me laugh to myself, the predictions rolling off my mind with the same ease as they were apparently rolling off my dad's.

Any upcoming surgeries weren't something to worry about. They were something to take in stride with confidence, knowing that we'd see the other side soon enough.

As for the doctors and nurses there, they might have been very knowledgeable; but they weren't ultimately in charge of that room or the room's occupant. There was a higher power in charge, and He was the deciding factor.

Don't Make It Mental

The bad news just wasn't working for Pop. Neither was the medicine, which he made clear after the nurses and doctors left.

"I realize the reports aren't looking good," he told me, "But I'm hopeful, and I prefer to be optimistic."

I was right there with him.

"You see, Michael," he continued, "these doctors are looking at the cup as half-empty and I'm looking at it as half-full."

All the while, *Rocky IV* played on in the background.

"I'm just going to listen to your mother and sisters from here on out. They're my winning team. So at this point in the game, I just want to hear the good news. My mind can't take any more of that negative mumbo jumbo."

Some would call it denial, I know. But that was just how my dad got when things weren't going well. He liked to focus on the positive.

"Don't make it mental," he would sometimes say if one of us was over-thinking a bad situation or if a negative thought was keeping us from focusing on a goal. And now it was our turn to remind him in the same exact way. He knew the family he and Mom had raised would lift him up after he'd been knocked so far down.

He also knew exactly where he needed to be to get back on track.

"Take me home back to my old stomping grounds," he told me. "It's time to get back to the basics. I'm going back into training, and it's time to make a comeback."

One of my dad's favorite lines after something big happened in the family was what he'd said after my sisters first left the room. "You couldn't write it any better if you tried." And this did seem to be one of those moments.

Here he was, flat on his back in a hospital bed on Christmas Day, talking about going back into training. Talking about how he was going to get up, beat the odds, and finish the race strong – all while *Rocky IV* continued on through its inspiring scenes as the tension in the room faded further.

SEVEN

When he fell asleep again, the credits were rolling, the final fight scene having finished. As I'd known to expect yet still looked forward to every time, Rocky had beaten the Russian, Ivan Drago. And he'd done it on Christmas Day.

CHAPTER 2
The First Lap

You couldn't write it better if you tried.

He awoke gently from "resting his eyes," already holding onto a new short-term game plan. "I've been napping and floating in and out of dreams all day," he declared. "I'm getting cabin fever. How about we go downstairs to where they have that piano in the lobby. It would be great to hear a little of your music."

That took me aback. It was the first time in my 17 years of playing that my dad had actually asked to hear me on the ivories. Most of the time, my playing was too loud, I knew. And since I was self-taught, my poor family had been forced to witness my slow and sometimes painful progression in the beginning.

I'll be the first person to admit that, in the first two years, I was downright awful. For the next five or so thereafter, I was only slightly painful. I suppose my older brother, Jimmy, best summed up my early years. After hearing me play one time, he said I should perhaps try learning guitar instead, adding in, "With the way you sound on that thing, your target audience is probably going to be sleeping babies and people hard of hearing."

Oh, a sibling's honesty.

SEVEN

My father, for his part, had never told me to stop playing, though I'm sure he may have wanted to do just that many times. So this was a big deal that he'd actually asked.

I checked with the nurse for permission first, and she gave me the green light, even helping me get him into a wheelchair. As I pushed him down toward the lobby, his face was drawn, but I could sense that his spirits were improving.

Seven Notes of Hope

Once we got to the piano, I positioned his chair right next to the brand-new and very shiny black baby grand sitting all alone in the corner.

"Can I look at the inside while you play?" he asked.

My answer was immediate. "You bet!"

I opened the huge lid so he could watch the strings reverberate as I hit the keys. Then I sat down and began to play a long, soft version of his favorite song, "What a Wonderful World."

It only took a short while before I could see his energy start to fade. He'd reached his limit for this excursion, I could tell. So I closed up the lid, unlocked his wheels, and we rolled back upstairs, both of us tired for very different reasons – yet a little lighter in spirit nonetheless.

According to Marianne, he later told her that, "Listening to that piano music was the start of my comeback."

Life Is but a Dream

As I pushed him back to his room, my father softly hummed a tune. Listening closely, I realized it was a familiar one: "Row, Row, Row Your Boat."

When he noticed me listening, he turned his head around to show the big smile on his face. "Life is but a dream," he informed me, then went right back to humming.

I started humming along with him, and we both laughed.

"They make these halls pretty long," he observed. "I could probably start my interval training here when I get back on my feet. It's like an indoor track!"

There was sheer delight in this childlike observation. I could sense he was regaining his strong mentality despite his physical weakness. So once we returned to room 313 and got him comfortably settled in, we started talking sports. The piano really had seemed to help bring him around and I recognized a new sense of peace within him.

Instead of fighting his present situation, he seemed to be surrendering to it with humility and grace. Though, if I knew anything about my father, he was also quietly biding his time for a very determined comeback. He might have been smiling out in the hallway while he talked about such things, but I knew he hadn't been joking.

A gentle knock at the door interrupted our conversation.

"Maybe your sisters have come back for round two."

We got a chuckle about that as the door slowly opened, though we knew it wouldn't be them. As he put it, they would never knock that softly. "They knock with thunder."

The Coach

That specific knock could only have come from one person, my mom, who entered the room with a visible glow around her. She gave my father a bright, loving smile as she moved to his bedside, an expression he returned beautifully.

"Well, looks like the coach has arrived," he declared, seeming to perk up further just looking at her. "It must be game time! Your mother can take it from here."

Mom gave me a hug. "They're all waiting for you at home. Marianne set aside a plate of dinner. You can put it on 300 for eight minutes."

Between those words and my dad's, I knew this was my cue to head home. So too was the way he turned to her to softly say how he'd missed her and was glad she was back.

"I missed you too, Dante." She gave him a kiss. "I'm here now, and everything will be fine."

As if to prove that life was already getting back to normal, she ran down the list of family updates. "The kids were asking for Pop-pop all day long. And Leah asked if Santa knew you were in the hospital. It was so cute how worried she was about you getting your gifts."

While she filled him in on the news from home, I gathered my things and got her situated in the chair next to the bed. But before

I could officially make my exit, Pop lifted his head from his pillow. The very sight made Mom light up. It was so reassuring to see. With a positive look on his own face, he chuckled a little bit. "Remember, Michael, if anyone asks how I'm doing, just tell them I'm pulling out of here to win!"

Thunder Road

My mind was racing as I drove down Interstate 95 toward our family home. On a normal day, I join the race of aggressive northern drivers and speed down that highway with the best of them. But today, I just took it easy and moseyed on my way in the slow lane.

I was thinking a lot. That and preparing myself for what I'd walk into, considering that the whole family was at the house. Going from a quiet hospital room to a house full of people made for an extreme difference, and I needed to steel myself to get in the right frame of mind.

As I drove, the sky looked like a Michelangelo painting made of snow-white clouds that were haloed by a burnished orange glow. The sun was setting on yet another Christmas Day.

As a kid, my sister Theresa and I would say we felt "bummed out" after the sun went down on December 25. We knew all the festivities were over once we went to bed, and that just felt like such a tragedy.

She would often lament, "I bet the sun doesn't want to go to sleep either. It probably wants to stay up just as much as we do."

If it was anything like me this year though, the sun was ready for bed.

The Long Way Home

I felt like I was psyching myself up for a race as I turned left onto my parents' street. Our family property, where I'd been born and raised, had seen so many races of all sorts throughout the years.

I guess these are the old stomping grounds my dad was referring to in the hospital.

That was my thought as I drove down the road and approached the big white fence that surrounds half our house. As I pulled into the driveway at "2121" – the abbreviated name we'd coined for the house – it looked like a used car lot. Between the trucks for the business and my parents' cars, the driveway usually looked full – but nothing like it did on this evening.

It reminded me of our fruit stand on a busy summer day. Cars were scattered everywhere in no particular order. Some were angled sideways. Some rested on the grass; some in the yard.

The exceptions to that haphazard arrangement were the five lined up at the top of the driveway. Those were perfectly arranged with almost military-precision, so I knew they had to belong to certain more "precise" sisters.

Since there was nowhere to park in the driveway, I decided to just hide my Jeep out of the way in the back field. As I stepped out into the cold winter's night, I buttoned up my jacket and put on my hat, perhaps in part as a distraction. It served as five more seconds to myself. I didn't know exactly what I'd be walking into, but I knew I'd have to answer a lot of questions.

Everyone would want a report – a very detailed one at that.

A Kitchen More Chaotic Than Grand Central Station

When I opened the front door, it sounded like I was about to walk into a busy coffee shop at its peak hour. From what I could tell standing on the porch, there were five different conversations going on in the kitchen.

That, in and of itself, was to be expected. Yet, as I was about to learn, my nieces, nephews and in-laws had already left and gone home for the night. It had been a long couple of days for everyone, and so the only ones who remained at the family headquarters were my seven sisters and three brothers. For the first time in years, it was just my immediate siblings together and they were all crammed into the kitchen like sardines.

As I composed myself on the porch, I couldn't help but feel like a coach getting ready to walk into a press conference after a game – with my siblings cast as the eager reporters, anxiously awaiting the play-by-play.

Cinderella Man

Upon entering the house, I first caught sight of Joseph, Dante and James; or Joey, Danny and Jimmy, as we call them. Joey was on his back under the sink, peering into the dark recesses and pipes below. I couldn't see his face, but it looked like he had mud and dirt all over his otherwise nice pants and shoes.

Danny and Jimmy, meanwhile, were apparently helping out with whatever venture Joey was currently engaged in. Soaking wet and somehow covered in dirt as well, they saw me come in but didn't say a word. They were too focused on the task at hand, which appeared to be quite involved.

Joey, of course, couldn't see me at all since he was still wriggling around under the sink. He'd put on about 30 pounds recently, which was rare for him at the time. While he'd outgrown all his shirts in the process, he didn't care enough to buy any new ones and just kept wearing clothing two sizes too small.

As such, trapped under the sink with his shirt halfway up his back, he looked like Gus-Gus in *Cinderella*, the adorably corpulent mouse whose belly always seems to be popping out of the bottom of his shirt.

That image aside, my brothers looked like they'd been through a domestic war of sorts. Apparently, the very cold weather had burst the pipes downstairs and now they were dealing with the ramifications… namely, the huge kitchen sink upstairs. To an outsider, it would appear as if they had walked into a food fight. This line of thinking would have been further fueled by the debris of food, glasses, empty wine bottles, and plates scattered everywhere.

For his part, Jimmy was standing on the counter above the sink with a plunger. Drenched in sweat and pumping the drain as hard as he could, he was clearly getting impatient. "Is that working?"

Joey, clearly not happy to be stuck under the sink in his Sunday best, was just as cranky. "No! Keep plunging! This damn pipe won't budge!"

So Jimmy kept right on pumping with the same intensity on his face as a miner digging for gold.

When You Need a Job Done Right…

As in so many other Italian households, my parents' kitchen was one of the most important rooms in our house growing up. So when Pop had it remodeled after Angela was born, he made sure to do everything right. And since about ninety percent of the furniture in our home was already Amish-made, it was no surprise when he chose his Amish buddy Abraham to remodel our kitchen as well.

One of my father's work territories was near Amish country in Central Pennsylvania, and he had made a lot of great friends in their various communities as a result. He loved their simplicity of life and unparalleled work ethic, so when it came time to build a new kitchen, he brought in the Amish-Team.

Even better than the four guys from the '80s TV show, my dad's 'A-Team' was comprised of a father and three of his eight sons. They were honest, hard workers, and very skilled at carpentry. Most importantly, my dad knew they'd get the job done right.

Half the Time at Half the Cost

There were plenty of contractors Pop could have hired to restore our kitchen, but he had his heart set on the best, no matter what it took to make that happen.

My family still teases him at times about the three weeks he spent driving over an hour every morning from Wilmington, Delaware, to Lancaster County to pick them up… and then the same distance bringing them back each night in our old family station wagon.

During that time, my mother of course made sure to feed them well. Perhaps that factored into how enthusiastically they did their work. (I wouldn't blame them if it did.) But one way or the other, they worked long hours and finished the job in half the time at half the cost because their prices were so fair. So maybe it was worth all that driving after all?

In the remodeling process, the only request Mom actually asked for was a bigger sink. She had cleaned dishes for an ever-growing family in her old puny sink for over 25 years without complaint, so it was easy to say that her time had come in this regard.

She deserved it, and then some.

In my father's usual fashion, he went above and beyond the call of duty in that department, working alongside Abraham to install two huge sink bowls. "I need to make up for all the years she only had one little sink," he joked, knowing that she probably deserved much more than that but settled for the best he could in 1984.

Brothers and Sisters

Now, almost three decades after the sinks were installed, Joey was uncomfortably squeezed into the cabinet below them, hammering away at the pipe as Jimmy plunged the drain from above. Danny, meanwhile, had his hand in the sink next to Jimmy, yelling orders to both of them.

It was like a modern day *Three Stooges* episode, where Joey was Curly, Danny was Moe, and Jimmy was Larry. None of them were on the same page and, to this day, I don't think any of them really knew what they were doing. They were just trying everything they could think of, cursing away as our sisters sat at the table, having a deep conversation and drinking wine.

The sink seemed to be the least of the women's worries. It was up to my three brothers to fix that particular issue, and my sisters weren't fazed at all by the swearing and yelling going on just 10 short feet away from them.

The whole scene was insanely impressive.

Sons of Thunder

"Joey! Turn it the other way!" Danny yelled, his exclamations laced with profanity. "You're turning it the wrong way!"

"No, Joey!" Jimmy was yelling over him. "It's going to bust if you keep banging it so hard!"

As for poor Joey himself, he had a knack for getting involved in any family crisis. Being the oldest sibling, it was no wonder his words and opinion held a lot of weight. Growing up, he was the house genius and leader of the pack in too many ways to count, so it came as no surprise he was chosen to fix this catastrophe.

Though perhaps he would have preferred to fix it on his own without Santa's two helpers above him. As it was, he was mumbling something in Italian and banging the pipe with a wrench.

Then, all of a sudden, the pipe burst.

Just like that, water started spraying everywhere, making it look like they had just struck oil as the endless spray went off in all directions. The top of the sink was shooting all the way to the ceiling, while the bottom was draining black liquid like a deranged bathtub faucet on full blast.

"Somebody grab some towels or a mop!" Jimmy yelled, hoping our sisters would see the situation was now in complete chaos.

It was a desperate cry for help: an S.O.S. that all hands were needed on deck to fix the now completely broken sink. My three brothers had started a flood, and it would take all eleven of us to stop the crisis.

That's not to say some of us couldn't see the humor in the situation though. Danny, for one, was laughing uncontrollably, shouting, "The Titanic is sinking! Everybody, jump! Women and children first!"

The children were already out, of course, and now that the women had finally taken notice of something other than their conversation, they weren't running away. Just the opposite, as all seven sisters jumped up from their seats to race to the disaster sight.

Everything but the Kitchen Sink

All 11 of us were running around, trying to help anyway we could. Patti, Denise and Linda were throwing kitchen towels on the floor while Theresa and Angela ran downstairs to the laundry room to get bigger shower towels.

Kate and I, meanwhile, grabbed the pots we cook our pasta in and started putting them under the sink. When one got full, she'd hand me an empty one, take the full one and pass it on to Marianne, who then ran outside to throw the water into the front yard.

The rest of the girls were now on their hands and knees, soaking up the water with their many towels. Paper towels, shower towels, kitchen towels and even sweatshirts were getting thrown to the floor. Anything that could soak up water was being put to use.

Danny, meanwhile, ran and got the vacuum out of the hall closet. "Don't use that!" Patti yelled as he turned it on and started sucking up water. You'll break it!"

But he wasn't to be dissuaded. "This is a disaster! I'm throwing in everything but the kitchen sink at this point." Still laughing hard, he almost couldn't get the wordplay out.

All 11 of us were running around trying to fix the spiraling-out-of-control plumbing problem. It was complete pandemonium and, for some reason, everyone was getting a kick out of it.

"You just have to laugh," Kate said as I handed her yet another full pot of water.

And we were. Everyone was cracking jokes as the sink kept right

SEVEN

on soaking the entire kitchen.

"You'd think out of 11 of us, someone would have married a plumber," Angela joked as she threw towel after towel onto the problem.

"If we'd all married Amish guys, we wouldn't have any of these problems," Linda laughed right back.

That was true, but I suppose we wouldn't have had that moment as a result.

Oh Brother

"I don't think they've cleaned that drain since they put it in back when Reagan was president," Joey said as he climbed out from under the sink again. "You'd think by this point, they'd invest in a garbage disposal."

The half-comical, half-incredulous look on his face summed up the entire situation. He was completely soaked now, with mud streaking his face, his shirt and his pants – more so than before.

Standing up, he took one look at his too-small top and ripped it off without so much as undoing the buttons, just like Superman ripping off his business suit to expose his famous caped spandex. The big difference, of course, was that Joey wasn't ripping off a business suit and flying up, up and away to save someone in a life-or-death situation. He was destroying one of the three actually nice shirts he owned, exposing a big round tummy in the process.

With her hands on her knees and already out of breath from laughing so hard, Linda managed to gasp out, "I knew there was going to be a big announcement this Christmas!" She had to struggle to get the rest out. "Joey's pregnant!"

We all lost it again, except for Joey, who crumbled up his shirt and threw it in the trash. It was difficult to tell what he was most perturbed by now: the fact that my parents never cleaned the sink to his standards or Linda's comment.

The rest of us thought it was hysterical.

Titanic Family Problems

Looking at Joey's stomach, it seemed like he was hiding a beach ball under his skin, an image that could amuse even the most saintly siblings. Which we were not.

Reaching for a cookie from the tray of baked Christmas goodies sitting on the counter next to him, Joey shoved it into his mouth. "Everyone take a good look because my New Year's Resolution is to lose 50 pounds. So get your laughs in now."

With that, he threw his hands into the air to yell, "I'm king of the world!"

As usual, his timing and tone were perfect.

Maybe it was a little mix of wine, general holiday stress, the mess in the kitchen and the fact that we were all deeply concerned about our ailing father, but Joey's line from *Titanic* immediately had us in stitches all over again.

The sink might have been done draining water, but now tears were pouring out of our eyes. It was like we were all having an emotional release at the same time and no one could control themselves.

Marianne and Theresa had to use the counter for support as they stood there laughing their heads off. Linda, Patti and Denise were quite literally rolling on the floor. And Kate, Angela and I were leaning on each other, trying not to fall over.

My stomach hurt, I was laughing so hard. It was a truly classic moment.

"You couldn't write it any better if you tried!" Jimmy yelled from the floor, where he lay in a fetal position, uncontrollably cracking up.

"So much for chestnuts roasting on an open fire or a silent night," Kate added. "This is our Very Brady Christmas, everyone!"

Just as things started to calm down, Danny went and weighed in one more time. "Not that it matters at this point, but I think I wet my pants."

And off we went again.

Take Me Home

Of course, it wasn't a Very Brady Christmas. This episode, unlike some TV show, wasn't going to be over in an hour. It was actually just beginning, and we were all trying to come together with the understanding that the road ahead for Pop would be a long one.

As much as everyone wanted a happy ending, the reality on this night was that we could lose our father. There was that undeniable potential, and we were all very aware of the fact. Yet we were also

SEVEN

aware that, no matter how much we tried to fix it, his story was in God's hands.

All we could do was sit back and prepare to be at our best since he was at his worst.

Since everyone was drenched from the sink situation, Angela grabbed sweatshirts for all 11 of us from the hall closet next to the kitchen. That way, we could at least be dry for the night's "second" Feast of the Seven Fishes.

The sweatshirts were the ones we wore for the Christmas business: red Champion products with a logo on the left side that read "Marini's" in white over a Christmas tree.

So there we all sat with our decades-old sweatshirts on while dishing out second helpings of dinner. It was reminiscent of the days before anyone got married and started having babies and families of their own.

As I looked around the table, I couldn't help but think how the conversations may have changed, but the scene was still the same.

The Press Conference

The kitchen usually looked like a war zone when the whole family was around. But on this night, it looked more like a tornado had touched down.

Also reminiscent of a whirlwind, my head was spinning a bit from the last two days – that particular evening included. But my sisters were ready for the report. And, of course, Linda was the first to fire off a question.

"So. Let's hear it, Michael. How did he look when you left?"

I put my fork down and picked up the glass of homemade wine I was having with my pasta. Theresa had poured me a very large glass since I guess she could tell I needed some added spirit. Everyone was feeling pretty good by then, but I still had a little catching up to do.

I took a nice, long sip and put the glass down to give them the best CliffsNotes version I could muster of the 21 hours I had spent with Pop.

"Last night, he was out of it when I got there, but he seemed a little better today. I think watching the *Rocky* marathon on TV made him happy."

That got some smiles.

"He was talking and telling some jokes too. Patti, you would have loved it. He actually quoted Bruce Springsteen when I was leaving. It was the last line from your favorite song, 'Thunder Road.'"

With that, everyone gave a half-hearted laugh.

"I think all the girls coming in to see him this morning really lifted his spirits. After all of you left, he was a new man," I went on honestly. "I do think he's going to be okay, and I know he thinks so. We went down to the piano in the lobby, and I played his favorite song for him."

Some interesting looks were exchanged among the female figures around the table.

"It only took 15 minutes before he was done," I continued. "So we went back up to the room. But he was happy to just get out for a little."

Recovery Mode

Finishing up that summary, I knew right away that I'd made a mistake. I'd gone into too much detail, which is never a good idea in a family with eight women. The looks I was getting from my sisters now reminded me of this.

They knew he should not have left the room for any reason, so I could see they weren't thrilled with that part of the report. Clearly, I needed to make a hasty recovery...

I took another sip of wine. "Look, he wanted to get out of the room for a little bit, and the nurse gave me the okay. I really think it helped him. He was humming the whole way back to the room."

Despite how that seemed to be settling better with them, I kept on going to see if I could dig myself further out of the doghouse.

"He definitely wasn't into the bad news from the doctors, and he needed a little lift. Sure enough, once we got back, he was really positive and said he was going to 'start training again' and make a comeback."

This time, my sisters all gave a simultaneous chuckle. They knew it sounded exactly like something he'd say.

"Maybe he can run his first marathon when he turns 80," Kate joked.

"Knowing him, he probably will," Theresa agreed.

"He wouldn't listen if we told him he couldn't do it anyway," Linda added while putting her feet up on the 13-foot table, showing off her fancy red Christmas socks in the process. She had just gotten them from her daughter, Madeline, who made them herself.

My slip-up aside, the mood at the table was pretty light considering everything that had recently transpired.

The Call

With the room falling silent again – a rare occurrence when we were all together – I continued with my report. "He doesn't like the guy scheduled to do his surgery. He wants Dr. G., and he made that very clear."

At one point during my dad's sleepy state between consciousness and dreamland, he'd made sure to tell me, "I want Dr. G. as my cut-man and in my corner for this fight." He was clearly not happy with his current doctor, who had wanted to perform surgery an hour after meeting him. From my dad's perspective, that surgeon just happened to have time in his schedule and was operating off of convenience alone.

I knew he thought he wouldn't make it off the operating table under that guy's knife.

Only focused on the positive part of what I'd said, Marianne lit up. "I'll call G.'s office first thing tomorrow. I know his schedule is crazy right now, but maybe he could fit him in sometime in the next two days."

Linda and Patti nodded their heads in approval. Linda, who was friends with the good doctor's wife, added in, "I know he would do it for him. He loves Daddy!"

The feeling was mutual. In my father's eyes, Dr. G. was the best man for the job at hand.

"If you guys can somehow get Dr. G.," I told them, "it will make all the difference to him."

With that, the decision was made. Marianne made a direct call to him early the next morning – "the call that saved my life," my father would later say.

Drafting All-Stars

Pop liked Dr. G. because he was "a nice Italian and a great family man." Two of my sisters had worked with him over the years, and he was also a customer of both the family produce market and our Christmas business. Anytime Dr. G. came to buy his tree and annual three wreaths, he would make a point of saying hello to my father, who was usually working in the empty house next door that had been converted into a workshop of sorts.

The only thing that could stop him from making wreaths all day was either an order for more material or a special visitor. And most of the time, he'd continue to work even when someone did stop by the loud and bustling wreath room to talk with him. But whenever Dr. G. would peek his head into the room, Pop would turn down his 1970s-era radio – which could only pick up one classical music station – to stop what he was doing and talk away.

It meant a lot anytime people gave us their business. But to my dad especially, it meant the world. He took pride in having the best quality products in town because, in his eyes, the customers "put food on the table for the whole family."

He was right about that too. They supported us, and the business supported the family.

Pop especially loved that Dr. G. would drive 45 minutes to our house to get his Christmas decorations every year. Plus, he appreciated the fact that their fathers knew each other from the "old country." They had come from the same town in the Marche region of Italy, a place named Ascoli Piceno. And anyone who knows the Italian community recognizes that kind of connection carries a lot of weight.

So once Pop heard that Dr. G. was going to take care of everything, he had no more fear. Even before that detail was set in stone, he knew my sisters would make it happen.

Like he'd said, his team was making the calls.

When it comes to the family, my sisters get things done. And when it came to getting help for our father specifically, they were at the top of their game. In less than 24 hours, everything was a go.

That Christmas evening though, looking around at my brothers and sisters, the last thing I said to wrap up the press conference was, "One thing's for sure: He's ready to get home to his old stomping grounds. And he is definitely pulling out of there to win."

CHAPTER 3
Lap Number Two

Keep your eyes on the fundamentals.

Pop was released from the hospital 10 days after first being admitted. Coincidentally, it was also New Year's Day.

He, of course, thought this was a great sign for his recovery.

Mom said that, when he left the hospital, he was holding the sunflower Theresa had brought him on Christmas Day, which was – also symbolically, perhaps – in full bloom.

The two sisters who were with him when he was rushed to the hospital in the first place were also there to bring him home. They said he was a little out of it when they left because he was on some heavy medication, but he kept mumbling something about it being "time to get back to the old stomping grounds."

Upon doctor's orders, he was not to have any visitors during the first few days after returning home. So he spent those days in bed, with Theresa's flower on the nightstand nearby. On a piece of paper, propped against the vase, he'd written a note to himself in big black magic marker that said, "Always remember THE BIG SEVEN!"

He didn't mention anything about it for days and days on end, and those days probably would have turned into months if not for one of my nephews.

Road to Victory

It was a cold Sunday afternoon in mid-January, about two weeks after he came home, when Marianne and Theresa brought their children over to see him, watch some football and eat Sunday dinner.

Marianne had four boys and a baby girl, while Theresa had three boys and a baby girl. The grandchildren had been over to visit a few times by then, but they never stayed long because of his weakened state. Now that he was feeling a little better, however, they were allowed to take up the whole afternoon.

This was a big deal.

Pop was in rare form on that particular day, and for good reason. If watching the Eagles beat the Cowboys on a perfect Sunday afternoon wasn't enough by itself, he was now able to enjoy it in the company of seven of his grandsons and three of his children out on the porch.

The Eagles' season was over and there were playoff games on the TV at the time, but Pop chose to watch a replay of the Christmas Eve game he'd missed back when he was fighting for his life. Due to the circumstances and our general love of everything Eagles, we were enjoying the grid-iron battle in front of us as if it wasn't already decided.

Mom had taken the babies, Leah and Italia, and put them in their Amish-made wooden highchairs in the kitchen so they could watch her make their favorite meal. That was tradition. She was a master in the kitchen, and the kids would sit in awe as she cooked for them.

My mother was especially known for making a mean grilled cheese and could do up to eight sandwiches at a time because of the size of the stove Pop put in when we remodeled the kitchen.

Lydia, the youngest of Linda's three daughters, once asked why her grilled cheese tastes so good. To which my mom responded, "Because they're made with love."

They really were. She loved to make them, and all the grandkids loved to eat them. Anytime they came to visit, that's what they wanted to eat and Mom was more than happy to oblige.

As for Pop, I knew he was in all his glory as he sat in his rocking chair with a grin on his face, cheering the Eagles at every play. After they'd score, he would start the famous Philadelphia chant…

Fly Eagles fly, on the road to victory!
Fly Eagles fly, score a touchdown one, two, and three!
Hit 'em low, hit 'em high and watch those Eagles fly!
Fly Eagles fly on the road to victory!

On Wings Like Eagles

My nephews were so excited. They hadn't seen their grandfather so happy since he'd been sick. Plus, everyone in the family is a huge Eagles fan, and the room was downright electric as the team outplayed the Cowboys up and down the field. Even though we were watching a recording of the game and we knew the eventual result, it was just as exciting now that we were all together watching it.

At commercial breaks, Pop would mute the TV to tell stories. That or recite poems, one of the uncanny abilities he happens to have. According to him, it was his one true talent in life, not to mention a very handy tool. The way he tells it, his poetic inclinations were what got him through grade school when the nuns would make them memorize and recite things from the Bible.

He'd never lost that tendency. And he used halftime to highlight it once again, turning the TV off altogether so he could share.

"I got a little poem I made up yesterday during my morning walk," he announced. "I'm going to call it *Late Kicker*. It goes something like this:

On this day, I am very clear
that some changes in my life are very near.
Just like in a race, I put my head down and go.
It's what the next lap brings that I do not know.

All I have is what's deep inside;
and with God as my coach, we run side by side.
When I used to run in races, I was never very fast at the start.
But I would soar like an eagle at the end
when it came down to heart.

He finished with, "I'm still working on it, but that's what I have so far. What do you guys think?"

Dusting Off a Classic

My nephews hung on Pop's every word anytime he spoke. In their young eyes, their Pop-pop could do no wrong and certainly not after fighting off death the way he had. They were all sitting near him in their own little Amish-made rocking chairs that he'd bought so they would never have to fight for seating.

The oldest nephew in the room that day was 12-year-old Alex, so they were all still innocent enough and unquestioning in the messages behind his stories. And that particular poem prompted Alex to beg his pop-pop to tell about when he won the first state cross country championship in 1953.

Since he and his siblings and cousins were all just starting their own running careers, they loved to hear tales about such things.

Marianne, Theresa and I had never heard much of his running stories over the years, so we were also excited to hear him now. Whenever he did tell running stories, they were usually about one of us, and he would never tell them in a bragging sort of way. In that last regard, this time was no different as he cleared his throat and began to tell the story in a humble voice.

"Oh yes, I remember how cold it was for that race," he began. "But I loved running in tough conditions. I won that race because of the good Lord and all the gifts he gave me to run across that finish line as the champion."

He turned the game back on, but the Eagles were winning by 13 points by then. So all my nephews wanted to do was hear more of Pop-pop's story.

"I used to LOVE the big races!" he said with a big grin on his face. "I never was very good at the beginning of the season; but as the big races approached, I'd start to really hit my stride. It was late October when they ran that first cross-country state championship out at Rockford Park…"

Catching Up to the Pack

"I was hoping for a cold day because I knew I ran my best in the cold," he continued. "And sure enough, it was."

He shook his head. "Before the race, I wasn't nervous. Not when I had faith it was in God's hands. I also had patience when it began and the pack went out really fast.

"Coming through the first half-mile, I was in the back of the pack, but I kept calm and stayed patient. I knew I would catch up as soon as things started to get tough after about one and a half miles."

The look in his eyes told us he was right back in the race. "The first half of the course was flat, but I knew there were two really big hills in the last mile, so my time would come to attack when it really mattered. No one remembers who wins the first mile. It's how you run the last that counts the most."

We all sat there, soaking up his every word.

"As the race went on, I wasn't tired," he explained. "I felt relaxed and at peace as I started to catch up to the leaders. And when I took the lead at the top of the final hill, 500 meters from the finish line, I felt joy in my heart and a spring in my step. I knew I had it."

His eyes sparkled. "I was soaring like I had Eagles' wings!"

With that, all my nephews started laughing.

My dad chuckled at his little joke too. "That's the story of how your pop-pop won the first state championship a long, long time ago. But I was just setting the tone for you guys. All of you will be way faster than I ever was."

By then, my nephews really didn't care about the football game. They had more questions, and they made it known.

Remembering that he had a picture from the race in his room, Marianne asked her second-oldest son, Benjamin, to go grab it out of his room. When he came back, he handed it to my father, who looked at it for a second with a smile.

"Yep, that's the picture," he affirmed. "Believe it or not, that's the only race my father – your great-grandfather – ever got to see me run in. He was always working when I raced, but he took off for this one.

"He knew it was a big one, and he didn't want to miss it. He gave up a whole day's pay, too, which was a big deal back in those days."

It was clearly a big deal to Pop even now, judging by the emotion in his voice. "If you look at this picture, you can see him standing at the finish line."

Everyone leaned in while he went on.

"I never saw him more excited in my life. Your great-grandfather was really proud of me that day. Even though he was usually very quiet and kept to himself, after the race, I heard him telling people in broken English, 'My boy! He-ah won the race.'"

My nephews smiled at that too.

"It was one of the classics," Pop reminisced. "It's the only trophy I ever kept through the years. The only one that really meant something to me when it meant so much to my father."

He started staring at the picture again, and it looked like he was tearing up a bit, which my dad rarely did. He's as old-school as they come in that regard, and I can count on one hand how many times I've seen him cry.

You could tell he was thinking back to that day though. Thinking about his father and how much he loved him.

I could relate.

How You Look at the Glass

Benjamin was very quiet and shy; so when he spoke, it was usually to express something important. When I saw he was about to say something, I figured it would be about the race.

Instead, he referenced the note he'd seen next to my dad's bed. "Pop-pop, what are the big seven?"

My dad let out a sigh of contentment. "Oh, you saw the little note next to my bed." Then he handed the picture to Theresa, explaining that what Benjamin had seen was in reference to all the gifts he'd gotten at Christmas from his angels who helped him in his time of need.

It was the big seven that got him home safe, he told them.

"Just like in that championship race," he tied it right back in, "I was an underdog in that hospital. But it didn't matter."

And thank God for that.

"It was humbling being in that bed with all those tubes in me, knowing there was nothing I could do to fix it. I had faith that the Lord would guide me though, no matter what the odds were against me. I hoped every day I'd be sitting here with you guys, watching the Eagles win."

None of us interrupted him to say as much, but in our hearts, all of us completely agreed.

"Patience got me through those long days when I just wanted to

SEVEN

get out of bed and run out of that place," he remembered. "I knew if I kept pressing on, I could and I would persevere in the end. I'd finish the race strong when it counted most."

We all hung on his words just as hard as before.

"I knew when I first got there that I was in the back of the pack. But I also knew I still had a big kick left in me." He took a drink of water from his Eagles mug. "See this mug here? It's half-full, not half-empty. As my father – your great-grandfather – would say, it all depends on how you look at the glass."

Gifts All Wrapped in Love

He put his mug down on the coffee table again. "It was all the love I felt from the cards you guys wrote me and all the hope the family brought when they came to visit that gave me peace in my heart. I knew if I could just get to the top of that hill, just like in the race, that I'd be sitting here with you guys today.

"When they wheeled me out of that hospital, I felt like I did when I was coming down the homestretch of that championship race. I felt a joy in my spirit and, even though I was in a wheelchair, I still felt a spring in my step. I knew I'd won, but only by the grace of God and the gifts He'd given me. The big seven gifts."

He paused to smile. "I mean, God is a busy guy. But He took mercy on me when I was in the hospital. He believed in me enough to keep me in the race and help me finish like a champion."

Noticing that the game was starting to get interesting again, my father turned the volume back up on the TV. But that didn't mean he stopped the conversation. "We all have the big seven, but sometimes we just forget they're inside us."

Right about then, my dad's eyes got glued to the TV as the Cowboys began to drive down the field.

"Did you ever forget the big seven?" nine-year-old Nicholas asked inquisitively.

Despite the action going on even at that moment, Pop turned the TV off altogether to address his grandson. "Yes, I think for a little while, I did forget. But this Christmas, I was reminded by your mommies and your aunts that I still had them in me. This Christmas, I got the big seven back and I will NEVER forget them again."

Will, Theresa's oldest son, piped up then. "What did Mommy

bring you, Pop-pop?"

My father's voice was soft and quiet. "She brought me love, William. She brought me lots of love and a blooming flower. That's how lucky I got this year. I got seven gifts all wrapped in love."

Top of the Mountain

Pop was slowly rocking in his chair, his grandsons rocking in their own miniature versions, as he took a deep breath. "You little guys may not see it the way Pop-pop sees it right now, but someday you'll all see what I mean. Stick to the basics, and just keep life simple. It was the gifts of faith, hope, love, perseverance with humility, patience, peace and joy that got me to the finish line, only by the grace of God."

With that off his chest, he looked around at everyone with a big smile. "Life is simple. Just remember that the good Lord is on your side, and anytime you're down, the big seven will lift you up and help you soar with eagle's wings."

He grinned. "When you need a lift, use a gift. Look at what they did for me! They took me from the valley to the peak. From the bottom of the mountain to the top."

He turned the TV back on then, this time for good. "Now, what do you guys say we watch the Eagles soar to victory!"

The Big Seven

The Eagles might not have made it to the playoffs that season, but one of their biggest fans was certainly set for a banner year. While his journey to full recovery wasn't always easy and the going wasn't always smooth, those gifts he'd been given back at the hospital didn't wear or tear as the days went on. They stayed constant, as the truest gifts tend to do.

Given by my seven sisters, they were testaments to seven unique lifetimes of nature and nurture that produced seven distinct personalities capable of such strength and encouragement.

That's what Pop saw on that Christmas morning, beginning with Patti and her "No retreat, baby, no surrender" Bruce Springsteen way of getting things done.

CHAPTER 4
Patricia: The Boss

Hope

My father said that, when Patricia – who we call Patti – entered the room that Christmas morning, she was "a wave of hope in a sea of despair." And Marianne told me it was Patti calling all the shots when he was first rushed to the hospital. Despite being at work when she got the news, Patti dropped everything so fast that she got there before he did.

It was Marianne and Linda who actually drove with him in the ambulance, stopping directly at the hospital's front doors when they arrived. But by then, Patti already had a team of medical professionals ready to go. Everything was prepared to the point where one doctor described her as "the General Patton of the hospital battleground."

Once they admitted Pop, my sisters took their leave, though only to return later that night. Linda said Patti came back into that room like a "raging bull in a ballet."

The way my oldest sister saw it, the room was filled with despair: the sense that death was expected, even inevitable. And since she had over 25 years' experience working in the medical profession as a nurse, she probably knew what she was talking about there.

Having Patti, Linda and Marianne on a medical team together was like having Joe Montana, John Elway and Dan Marino on the same team for the Super Bowl. But Patti especially didn't hesitate to set things right in the most blatant of ways. Within 30 minutes of arriving that second time, she had our father moved into a room of his own.

Marianne says she thinks it was closer to 10.

As our father later put it, "God prepared her for that moment all her life." Patti knew exactly what he needed, and that wasn't to share a room with another patient who was loud and spreading bad energy. So right up to the floor's head nurse she marched.

"Our dad is fighting for his life, and he needs quiet right now. I saw an empty room in 313, and the hospital is only 70% full. Is there any way you could help us out here?"

With that, my father was moved from the small room with no window and a loud roommate – to his own space with a beautiful view of the city lights in the distance.

Patti sat with him that entire night.

Patti at Her Best

As a kid, I used to look at her as some kind of Hollywood star. Certainly, she was the person who took my younger sister, Angela, and I to our first Bruce Springsteen concert. And she was the awesome big sister who treated us to Disney World for the first time.

There never seemed to be a dull moment for her, and her ability to help out in any situation, whether inside or outside the family, was awe-inspiring.

Patti is a natural "fixer," both in her life and her career as a nurse. She's just that type of person, giving the best she can one way or another. With her huge heart, I guess that sort of thing just comes naturally.

It may have a little to do with the fact that she's the oldest female in the family and second oldest of the entire gang. But I think it's more than that. I think she was given that gift well before she ever realized her order in the family.

She's been in the middle of many a family situation through the years, whether rescuing some of our sisters out of rough spots or stepping in to smooth out major events in any of our lives.

Patti is the backbone of the family in so many ways.

SEVEN

Out of my many siblings, she's probably the one who could write a best-selling book about her life – something inspirational and empowering that makes readers feel like they can do it too. She is a Manifesting Generator, a specific kind of person who is focused on putting the world to right. So wherever she goes, action is bound to follow.

Patti is also the sister who taught me the most about the strength of a woman's spirit, not to mention human perseverance in general. Since I was so young when she went through most of her growing pains, I got to watch and learn a lot. And, to my recollection, she never showed it whenever she was going through difficult times. Almost all my memories of her growing up are of her being happy.

Maybe I've just chosen to forget the bad ones. Or maybe Patti is just the kind of person who turns lemons into lemonade.

The Family's Underboss

Every family has one: the one person in the group who's brought in to deal with the big issues. If something important is happening or big decisions need to be made, that's the family member they go to… kind of like the reliever coming out of the bullpen in baseball, the enforcer in hockey or the striker in soccer… right at a crucial part of the game.

In *Pulp Fiction*, when an impossible situation needed to be fixed, they had "The Wolf." In my family, we had Patti. She was our big hitter in the bottom of the ninth. The sibling called in for special missions.

Put her in the picture, and boy, would she come through. There was no question about it.

One time, when one of my sisters thought her boyfriend was cheating, Patti proceeded to sit outside his apartment and wait for him to come home.

Most people would have gotten bored like that, but not her. She had a purpose and a plan, which entailed her waiting right up until he came along, arm in arm with another girl. And then she went to confront him, letting him and his date know she knew the score.

That guy never willingly showed his face around my family after that. Though, whenever my other sisters would see him out and about, they'd make sure to wave.

Just because they could.

In short, Patti is simply not the type of person who sits around until someone else gets things done. It's not in her nature. She's the type of person who'd much rather do it herself.

That's a trait all of us siblings have to a certain extent, but no one more then her. When our family has to go to battle to deal with any crisis, Patti has made a habit of being on the front lines calling a lot of major shots.

If my family was in the Cosa Nostra – the Sicilian Mafia – she would most definitely be the underboss.

Seeds of Hope

That makes her sound scary, I know. And, admittedly, getting in her way when she's on a mission isn't advised. But she's so much more than her take-no-prisoners mantra.

It was Patti, after all, who introduced me to Bruce Springsteen and the idea of chasing your dreams no matter the odds. This was especially true when I was a kid. She had this inexplicable way of planting seeds of hope in my head about life's amazing possibilities, including ones I had yet to see or even dream up in my mind.

Whatever she said was like nuggets of gold in my mind. They were resources to be invested and reinvested. So that's precisely what I did – with amazing gains to show for it. She never seemed short of pearls of wisdom or encouragements either, always ready with something else for me to consider whenever we would pal around.

And there was no one better to pal around with than Patti.

Being the oldest girl and second-oldest child made her into a trailblazer in the family. She was the first to go to prom, date boys, dress in the latest fashions and move away after school. Whatever Patti did, she did it the only way she knew how: Patti's way.

Nothing seemed to bother her. If a boy broke up with her, it was his loss. If she failed a test, she would just let it roll off her back, turn around and ace the next one. She knew how to handle things, both good and bad.

Patti, Bruce and Me

Patti always looked after me as a kid. When the house got too chaotic, which it did a time or two in a family of 13, she would take my hand and walk me out to the car. Then we'd go out driving with Bruce playing in the air around us. Nothing but Springsteen would come out of Patti's tape deck in the car or radio in the house.

It was a staple I could always count on. Just like her.

One Bruce song after another would blast from the speakers as she told me story after story about the big world I had yet to see. Springsteen set the tone during our "daydream drives" and, looking back, I wouldn't have it any other way. He sounded off the perfect notes for our little trips.

Since I was the youngest child in the family for seven years, it took me a while to make sense of some of the big-kid drama going on around me. But when Patti was around, she'd put everything in perspective, ending with words to guide me.

"Never let go of hope!" she'd say. "You have to hope and dream all the time."

Taking that in, my young heart would fill with excitement and my head with daydreams about everything life still had in store for me.

"This is just the beginning," she'd assure. "It keeps getting better and better."

Playing Hooky

"Are you sure it's okay we left without telling anyone?" I asked Patti as we sped off in the silver '79 Catalina five of my siblings shared at the time. They called it "the Jag" because my brother had put a Jaguar decal on the hood. "I hope we don't get in trouble."

"Don't worry about it, Mikey!" she said with the most reassuring voice. "It's fine. If we told everyone we were leaving, everyone would want to come. I mean, they all want to ride in the "cool car, you know."

"What's the "cool car?" I asked.

"Any car you're in!" She cast me the most contagious smile. "Since you're captain of the cool car, you decide where we go today."

"Can we go to the toy store?" I asked while the wind blew back my curly black hair, which was so thick it made my head look huge, earning me the nickname of "Snow Cone Head" from my cousins.

Cut twice a year, I never combed it because it simply could not be combed. The only thing that would make it move was the wind when I had the windows down going 50 mph or more.

"Of course we can, captain," Patti agreed. "And on the way back, how about we stop by Lickity Split?"

No wonder I knew Patti was awesome even at such a young age. Suggesting ice cream was a perfect idea in and of itself. Of course. But suggesting ice cream from the shop with the best custard in town was sheer genius.

So were her next words.

"Then we can get some ice cream for everyone so they won't be upset I took the car. Just hold on for the ride and let that mop of yours blow in the breeze." Shaking her head, she grinned. "That thing really is out of control, Mikey."

We both laughed as she put her foot on the gas.

Patti had her sunglasses on, and her hair was going everywhere like it did when she would blow dry it. She'd just turned 21, and she seemed to have not a care in the world as she drove with one hand on the wheel and the other hanging out the window.

As for me, I was so excited to be driving around like a free bird. Especially with Patti. She was like the female version of James Dean in my eyes. James Dean playing Bruce Springsteen from her speakers. Really loud.

It was perfection. Sheer perfection, Patti-style.

As we drove, she'd explain the songs to me, often at my request.

"What's this song about, Patti? What's a thunder road?"

"It's one of my favorite songs," she said. "It's about letting your hair down and following your dreams in life. Everyone should listen to this song when they drive."

"Why do you always listen to the same guy," I asked next. "Don't you like anyone else?"

That got raised eyebrows. "This is Bruce Springsteen. Is there anyone else?"

As we drove, we would talk about all types of fun stuff, from the Phillies, to the places she wanted to visit around the world, to how much we loved to drive around. We would just dream the day away as we passed the faces and places in our hometown.

From One Animal House to Another

Patti's life and attitude have always fascinated me. Back when I was five years old, I would see her coming and going to this "college" place. Since she went to school a mere 30 minutes from our house, she would often come home for quick visits, leaving me to wonder where she was off to as she walked out the door.

My imagination expanded significantly when I thought of what "college" might be like. It must be a good place – even a great one – when Patti always seemed so happy to go back to it.

One of the most classic college movies of all time, of course, is *Animal House*. Featuring a fraternity filled with different characters and different quirks, it's like a zoo for people, a concept most big families can relate to. The more kids you add to the picture, the more of an "animal house" you get, minus the boxed-in classes.

That's not to say you don't still get an education. Just that the lessons you learn each day aren't necessarily going to be neat and orderly, or scheduled.

Joey would tease my sisters when they left for school that they were just going from one animal house to the next. It was a statement I never quite understood until I actually stepped foot on a real-life college campus at the tender age of six. And yes, it was all thanks to Patti.

"Hey, Mikey, do you want to go meet my college friends?" she randomly asked one day. "We can get out of this animal house for a bit."

Without a second of hesitation, my shoes were on and I was ready to go, barely able to contain my excitement.

College

Bruce Springsteen's "Jungleland" was blasting as we drove down the driveway, with Patti in the driver's seat and my Incredible Hulk action figure sharing shotgun with me. We were on our way to college!

"Are we almost there yet?" I wanted to know within no time at all.

"We'll be there in half an *Incredible Hulk* episode," she assured.

As a five-year-old, that was how I told time: by comparing it to my favorite TV pastime. An hour's drive was one *Incredible Hulk*. A half-hour's drive was half an *Incredible Hulk*, and so on.

Just because I understood her answer didn't mean I was any less excited though or any less curious about what I'd find. I asked her question after question while we sped down I-95.

PATRICIA: THE BOSS

"Where do you eat?"
"Do you watch TV there?"
"Do you play with your friends after school?"
This barrage continued until we arrived.
"Take a look, Mikey," she told me. "This is my college."
Since I was short enough to be able to actually stand on the front seat, I ripped off my seatbelt to do just that. I can still remember that first image of "college." It was a beautiful spring day, and all the birds were chirping. Young people were riding around on their bikes, hanging out on lawns, throwing frisbees around. Some were walking; others were running. But everyone seemed to be going somewhere or doing something that looked like lots of fun.

With that, I got it. There was no need to say another word. I understood now.

No wonder Patti got so excited to come here! It was like going to the carnival minus the rides.

Was it recess, I wanted to know, since so many people were running around playing instead of being in class? But she said that college didn't have recess. College wasn't like school at all.

Taking everything in with wide-eyed wonder, I had to agree. It was more like an extended recess in my mind.

"So this is where you go when you leave the house to go to school?" I didn't wait for a reply. "This is way better than my school!"

My school didn't have big buildings, stores and fields to play in. And it definitely didn't have an ice cream shop.

It was at that moment I decided this "college" land was one of the coolest places in the world. I could not wait to go when I got older.

Anywhere with food, fun and ice-cream was where I wanted to be.

A Glimpse of "Heaven"

"You're TBMOC today, Mikey!" Patti said as we strolled through the plush grass outside the student center.

I looked at her, puzzled.

"You're the big man on campus," she explained. "All my friends can't wait to meet you."

With those words – never mind reality – I officially felt 10 feet

SEVEN

tall. It was like Charlie seeing the chocolate factory for the first time.

In my young, Patti-awed mind, I was as close to Heaven as I'd ever been before.

For me, that day was off the charts. But for Patti, having my back in such a fun, inspiring fashion was just how she lived. That's why, in my book, there's simply nobody in the world like her.

Shining Star

There we were.

All 13 of us. The entire immediate family. On a stage made for a five-piece band.

For the record, the five-piece band was also front and center up there on the platform, playing away while my parents, seven sisters, three brothers and I danced around the stage. The song that had prompted us up there in the first place was a Bruce Springsteen song, which we felt we needed to especially celebrate in honor of The Boss.

Him and Patti.

It was the night of my little sister Angela's wedding. With the seventh girl in the family now officially married, my family was letting loose regardless. But when that particular song came on, none of us objected one bit as Patti led us up on stage while the saxophone player played right toward her. It was almost like Clarence himself, Springsteen's one-time saxophonist, was speaking to her.

I've never seen her so happy. As Linda later said, "She was glowing!"

It may have been Angela's wedding that day, but the spotlight was on Patti in that moment. In fact, the bride had requested the song in honor of the Springsteen concert she, Patti and I went to at the old Spectrum arena in Philadelphia in 1999.

That had been a classic night, without a doubt. But it couldn't hold a candle to this one. And there was no better person to lead the family in our final female wedding dance than Patti.

Pulling Out of Here to Win

It was only fitting that it was my little sister, my oldest sister and

PATRICIA: THE BOSS

I who gathered everyone together to rush the stage as Springsteen's "Rosalita" played at the end of the reception. Truly the highlight of all Marini weddings! We were ending on a high note, with the whole family crammed on the little stage, dancing and singing like never before.

The band loved it too. Pop was wearing a white hat straight out of *The Godfather*, which may have been why the musicians asked us to stay on stage for the final song of the evening: "Don't Stop Believing" by Journey.

When that song played at the very end of the final episode of *The Soprano's*, everything faded to black. But with my family, the lights were oh-so bright. Everyone was beaming, and in the middle of the sunshine stood Patti like a ray of light through the heart of our family.

She really is as cool as James Dean and plays her best music under the brightest lights, just like Springsteen. And no amount of darkness can truly stop her.

None.

It's said that the last sign at the entrance of Hell reads, "Abandon all hope." And that may be. But when our father was in his darkest moment, it was hope that took charge.

It was Patti.

Our Father in Heaven will always be that wave of hope in a sea of despair. It's just that, sometimes, he uses people to send that wave. People like Patti.

CHAPTER 5
Denise: The Champ

Patience

When my sisters came to see my father that Christmas morning, it was Denise who brought him a poem. One of his favorites, it was called *The Game of Life*, and she hung it above his bed.

That was beautiful, but Denise brought so much more than that reminder. She also brought a sense of patience, which she went on to spread throughout the room. Cheesy sounding or not, she brought patience for the patient, which he desperately needed.

Pop was at a definite and obvious low point, yet Denise arrived with a game plan to get him through it. She figured out the number of different tests they were running on him and how many days he would be in the hospital. And she also had a plan for him to get back on his feet, all of which she set out in front of him. Just like a coach putting a race strategy together, all the information was mapped out.

Essentially, my sister was telling him to have patience. It wasn't time for him to make any big moves, and she kept reminding him he was right where he needed to be.

It's only fitting that message came from Denise. No one can talk to him like she can, and he needed her calmness especially right then, complete with her reassurance that he'd get another chance in the race of life.

Just like a coach might advise a runner not to give it all they have right away, Denise told him to, "Sit back now, have patience and, when the time is right, you'll know when to make the move." It was something he could appreciate, this strategizing of his recovery in the same way he used to map out racing strategies.

Leader of the Pack

As already mentioned, my family has its share of runners. And all of us competed in track and field or cross-country in high school. It just seemed natural the way running fit my family so perfectly.

Pop described racing in a very simple way, calling it the truest test of the mind, body and spirit. He preached the basics, along with ways to be a winner, on a daily basis in our home. Most things, he said, could be applied to anything in life; but running stood out especially.

Certainly, it helped instill in us a strong sense of our family's work ethic in our early years. And it kept us in good shape to work the long days at the family businesses as we grew up.

Running is a simple sport, though not an easy one. It's also not necessarily about who has the most talent. It's about who has the most inner fortitude to fight through pain, and it's about who can push themselves past it.

Really, running is a primitive sport. So much so. Just line a bunch of people up, say "Go!" and the first one to the finish line wins. The end.

But for as primitive as it is, it contains so much future-building potential. Patience and perseverance separate the good runners from the great ones. That's true both on and off the track.

And in that regard, Denise was the leader of the pack.

Rain, Sleet or Snow

Denise was the one who led the way and set the bar when it came to our father's training philosophy. I have so many memories of her being all bundled up in her running gear to head out the door for yet another practice run. No matter the weather too. Rain.

SEVEN

Sleet. Snow.

It couldn't stop her.

No wonder then that it wasn't just her family she outpaced. Denise was also a seven-time state champion in our Small Wonder State of Delaware. There are so many stories to tell about her running career, but above all, I remember watching in awe as she so gracefully won race after race after race.

One thing I knew when I watched her let loose: Everyone else was going to be fighting for second. Because Denise was coming in first.

The Making of a Champion

Denise's endurance and tenacity enabled this naturally quiet girl to transform into a ferocious competitor. In short, when she ran, she ran to win. No matter that she wasn't the biggest or the strongest, she was the one willing to outwork anyone.

It was a work ethic she brought wherever she went.

During the Christmas business, for example, when everyone was tired after a 13-hour day and ready to quit, Denise would still be in her little corner, creating our famous Cabbage Patch Trees – the little handmade trees my father invented in 1984 when Cabbage Patch Kids were popular.

No matter the task, she went above and beyond the call of duty. Even with a full-time job running her own therapy business, Touch of Health, she still managed to lead by example whenever the hectic holidays began.

Rookie of the Year – Seven Years Straight

Every new Christmas season that rolled around, Denise knew her roles, both the ones she took on herself and the ones assigned her.

Each of us had specific tasks to do during the holidays, most of them set in stone. For me though, as a kid, I had a lot of different "jobs." Dozens of them, actually. Most being the ones that no one else wanted to do.

That little detail was usually obvious enough, particularly after the holiday business cycle was done and over. When all of us were lounging around, totally exhausted on Christmas day, we'd give out all types of awards to each other. My award for seven years straight was "Rookie of the Year" because each year seemed like the first one I'd ever worked a particular job.

My family would joke each season's end that it was my first year actually working.

I'd like to think I was such a stealthy worker, and that's why no one noticed me. But the truth was that everyone was so busy during December that it was easy to get lost in the holiday shuffle. So, for seven straight years, I was considered a rookie.

Being older, my brothers all had their jobs secured. Joey did the wreaths, Jimmy decorated the cemetery arrangements, and Danny made the cemetery arrangements. These were used to honor the Italian tradition of paying respect to those who passed by placing a gift on their graves. It was my grandfather who started that particular tradition back when he first came here from Italy, making the memorials for close friends and family.

Today, we use the same arrangements he did back then. It was therefore quite the honor to do the same job he once had.

My jobs, admittedly, were a little less prestigious – more along the lines of keeping the potbelly stove going, keeping the floors clean and making sure that everyone had enough greens on their work tables. My dad called me the "cut man" because I did so many tasks that largely went unnoticed.

But he also made sure to tell me that my most important job was to make sure all my brothers and sisters had everything they needed to make the business run smoothly.

I took that charge very seriously. Though not as much as another task I was assigned to. To me, this other year-round responsibility wasn't even a task.

It was a calling.

The Human Hanger

Although we technically had two family businesses that I worked at growing up, the job closest to my heart didn't have anything to do with produce or Christmas trees. It was much more related to running.

You see, I was the official holder of Denise's warm-up suit on race day. And, boy, did that make me feel important!

Before each race, I'd run down onto the infield and grab her sweats as she was stepping to the line. It was sometimes a challenge to get there without being noticed, because only coaches and runners were allowed on the track for the big meets. However, the thing was, she never took her sweats off until the very last seconds before a race. She wanted to keep her legs warm and ready right up to the gun.

As soon as she shed her sweats, she was ready to fly. So one way or the other, I needed to get there.

Mere seconds before the gun would fire, Denise would take off her topmost layer of clothing and I'd be there, ready to catch them when she tossed them my way. While she ran around the track, I'd hold and protect that sweat suit like a Secret Service agent guarding the president.

How I loved being a part of her process!

Nature's Call

It's here I have to admit how I made a tragic mistake before one of her greatest races. It's one I'll never live down in family folklore.

I was in kindergarten at the time, which meant I didn't have the same ability to analyze situations, choices and potential consequences as I do today. So I may or may not have downed three too many Italian water ices at the concession stand, after which I really had to use the bathroom.

This wouldn't have been a big deal except that it was right in the middle of Denise's final County Championship high school race, where she was going for the 3,000-meter county title as well as the state record. Yet, wouldn't you know, nature called right about then.

I did report for duty on cue to serve as the "human hanger" of her clothes. At least there's that. Yet it wasn't too long after the race began that I could barely move.

After lap two, I had to go so bad I was dizzy. So I dropped her sweats and ran behind the concession stand, where there was a clear line going into the bathroom. Seeing me disappear, my mom ran to get me, not wanting to leave me alone. And she stayed with me the whole time the line moved ever so slowly forward.

While I finally made it into the actual bathroom without incident, I could hear her outside the whole time, urging me to hurry up while I tried to take care of business as quickly as possible.

I knew that I'd left my post and that I wasn't doing my very important job. But in my little brain, I also knew I would have wet myself on the infield if I'd waited until the end of the race.

A 3,000-meter run, even by a champ like Denise, isn't short.

Sweet Relief With Pangs of Guilt

"Hurry up, Michael," Mom begged. "She's starting her kick!"

But I just wasn't done yet.

Next, I heard, "She's on the last lap. Please, Michael! Hurry up and finish so we can see her cross the line!"

I could hear the desperation in her tone while I tried to finish my big-boy business.

"I think she may get the record, and I don't want to miss it!"

There Denise was, ready to set the state record in the 3,000-meter run. And there I was, standing with my pants down to my knees in sweet physical relief while feeling simultaneous pangs of emotional guilt.

Long story short, my mother and I were the only two people there who missed the race's climax.

We could hear the announcer on the loudspeaker telling everyone to cheer Denise on. I was in midstream when he told the stadium, "Look at her go, folks! She has a chance to get the state record! She is really flying now!"

And I could hear the crowd roaring in response as I was trying to finish.

I was missing it all, and so was my mom. Even truly trying to follow my mom's commands to "go faster," I didn't make it back to my post in time. Like they say, "When you gotta go, you gotta go."

As it turned out, deserting my post didn't change a single thing. Because even while I was "going" for it, Denise was rounding the track to set that state record, just as predicted.

Going to the Big Show

Denise was always patient in her races, taking her competitors down like a predator hunts its prey. She would make a noticeable effort to hold a modest position – until just the right moment. And when just the right moment came, she'd make her move.

The stadium would become electric at that point. No one could stay with her when she kicked it into high gear! And people knew it. They recognized that they were witnessing greatness when my sister ran.

Like a racehorse, she had a nose for the finish line. There was no two ways about it… She simply crushed the local competition. So after her senior year in high school, she decided to give the rest of the country a try and enter in the AAU Junior National Track Meet.

Early to Rise

It was only three days after Denise won the state title (her seventh) in the 3,000-meter that I got a literal wake-up call from my father. He slowly tiptoed to my bedside, shook my mattress a little and told me to put on my sweat suit.

I thought for sure I was in trouble. My dad never came in to wake me up, especially not at 5:47, which was way too early to be getting up for school. Way too early to be getting up for anything, actually, in my kindergarten mind.

Yet up I got after he told me he needed my help with something. I didn't even ask what it was. I could tell by the excitement in his eyes that it wasn't work related.

Springing out of bed, I put on my favorite all-green running sweat suit. For the record, it looked like something a mafioso might be caught wearing in an FBI surveillance photo, though I didn't recognize it at the time.

As I rushed into the kitchen, my father was sitting at the table with Denise intently listening to his every word. Neither of them noticed me at first. They were both busy reading something important from my father's "notebook of knowledge." It was his book of secret workouts and training strategies he referred to for the most important events.

Denise was eating a banana and drinking juice. He had no food in front of him at all, a sight I had never seen at our kitchen table.

I sat down next to her. She seemed intently focused, but once she saw me, she let out a big smile.

"You think you're ready for this, Mikey?"

Though I still didn't know what she was talking about, my immediate answer was "yes." If Denise and running was involved, then so was I.

DENISE: THE CHAMP

All Business

The house was quiet, what with the rest of the family still tucked away in bed. Only a small light was on in the kitchen, and my father and sister spoke in soft whispers as they rose from the table to head out the front door.

Denise had her running gear on, and as soon as her foot hit the first step, she was off on her morning training run. This was something I had long-since become used to with Denise. By the time I was getting up, she'd be coming in from her run to eat breakfast or do homework at the table.

Admittedly, I was often a bit on the tardy side those days. We were supposed to leave for school within 10 minutes of each other, yet many a morning, she'd be stuck taking me because I missed the bus. Again.

That meant I'd be shoved in the car, surrounded by three of my sisters and two of my brothers, getting an earful because of my lack of timeliness. Denise however, clearly, didn't have such issues.

Pop used to tell us that it was the early-morning runs while your competition slept that made the real difference on the final lap. In which case, Denise was no doubt well ahead of them all.

He and I watched her run off into the darkness, flying into the dawn of the day with grace and beauty. It was a mild morning that was perfect for running, which, in turn, made my "mafia sweat suit" perfect as well. Though I did find myself wondering why my sister didn't sleep in and enjoy the fact she'd just become a seven-time state champion days before.

Pop and I followed behind her at a much more leisurely pace, crossing the street to St. Edmond's track, which can be seen right when you step out onto our front porch.

"Denise really wanted you to come with us today," he told me with a gleam in his eyes. "She asked for you."

"Me?" That surprised me a lot. "What does she want me to do, Daddy?"

He handed me his old-time stopwatch that his college coach, Ken Steers, used back in the '50s. "She's doing a very important workout today, and she wants you to stand on the backstretch to yell out her time."

My job was to call out the time – her split – as she came by the 200-meter mark, which was her mid-mark. Or, as my old-school dad would have it, the 220-yard mark.

It's Biblical

This particular workout was going to be one of the hardest ones she'd ever done, Pop told me.

"Why is she doing such a hard workout?" I asked with great concern.

"Because she's training to race the best in the country, and she needs to be ready. It's time to put the hay in the barn."

An Amish friend of his introduced him to that expression, and ever since then, he loved to say it whenever training season came around. The way he saw it, as long as you've worked hard and put the hay in the barn, you'd be ready at harvest time.

Since my father was a farmer himself, many of his quotes – when not about running – related to working hard and being ready when the time came to reap what you'd sown. "It's biblical!" he would often add after he told us those pieces of advice.

Sure enough, they were scriptural. Practical too. Farmers who didn't get up early to do the little jobs were bound to regret it later. "The field must be prepared long before the rain," he would tell us. "There's nothing worse than getting to the big part of the season and not being ready."

That applied not just to farming, but running too. And not just to running, but life in general.

220s, 440s and 880s

As my father went over the instructions of what I needed to do, Denise appeared in the distance. The sun was slowly coming up over the trees that surrounded the otherwise shadowy track. I knew Marianne and Theresa, my roommates at the time, would be opening their eyes soon enough, wondering where I could possibly be at such an early time of day.

Little would they know.

Once Denise got up to us, she began to take off her sweats, handing them to me as she did. She didn't say a word, but the look in her eyes was pure fire. The task ahead? She was clearly going to take it on.

Even so, I couldn't help but feel nervous for her, knowing how she was getting ready to run such a tough workout. And all by herself too.

Not that I was going to tell her any of that. Not with that aura about her.

Pop told me to go to the 220 mark – an eighth of a mile, in his old-school language – and start the watch as soon as I heard him whistle. Nobody had to tell me what he meant by that last part. There'd be no shiny metal instrument involved, just a pinky and index finger strategically placed to his lips. My whole family very well knew the piercing sound he could make on his own, which he used whenever it was time to eat and he wanted everyone in the kitchen.

As for me, I sprinted across the field to my post, feeling like I was getting ready to run a race myself.

Now that the sun was up, I could see Pop giving Denise some final instructions, with her nodding her head in agreement. The next thing I knew, my father's famous whistle was piercing the air and I was starting the watch.

There was no hesitation whatsoever as Denise took off like a filly out of the gates at the Kentucky Derby.

With complete ease, she rounded the first turn to breeze down the backstretch. Each step covering ground. Running on her toes. Getting closer to me.

As she passed, I stood in such utter amazement that I forgot to yell out her time. She was in enough of a zone though that she didn't even notice, too busy blowing by me like a ghost in the morning light, rounding the turn and heading down the homestretch.

After she finished, she jogged a bit, then got right back on the line.

Pop whistled, and I hit the clock. This time, I'd do my job. I was determined.

Again, she floated the first turn and blazed the backstretch. "That's it, Denise! You look great!" I yelled, meaning every word. "You can do it!"

Sure enough, she was.

"Thirty, thirty-one," I called out on cue as she blew by me.

On the other side of the track, Pop was calling out his own encouragements, telling her to stay relaxed.

Once again, she finished and took about 60 seconds to herself.

Then, just like a boxer, she got right back to the line. Lap after lap, she glided with such ease that I started to feel sorry for the "best girls in the country" she'd soon be racing.

There were officially no more nerves left when it came to my opinion of how she was going to do.

Seven Down, One to Go

After seven such intervals, Pop waved me over to him, and I took off across the field. My little legs could barely keep up with me.

"This is her last one," he explained, "so make sure you really cheer loud. She's tired, and she needs to hear you."

With that, I ran back to my post for the final interval. Pacing back and forth, I could see my father pacing as well.

Denise toed the line one more time, my father whistled one more time, and off she went again. The sun now covered half the track, and I could really see her flying.

"You got it, Denise!" I shouted. "You can do it!"

She pounded closer.

"You're doing great!"

On, she went.

"Twenty-nine. Thirty. Thirty-one!"

As I yelled her time, she looked at me and winked. It was an awesome moment for me, hyped up on how amazing my sister was and how cool I felt for being a part of her process.

She was running a sub-60-second pace, and doing it with such ease that it looked like she was on a Sunday stroll in the park. I was so excited that I began screaming at the top of my voice, "Go, Denise!! Go!!"

I could hear Pop much more calmly coaching on the other side of the track, "Hit light... Nice and easy... Get on your toes..." And then, much more loudly, "Just hit light and float!"

That was a familiar line from him. It was his way of telling us to be loose and just fly with no effort, a reminder to float on air when the load seemed heaviest.

With that encouragement, Denise did exactly that. She got on her toes, hit light and flew through the finish line. Personally, I was so excited that I ran around the track, making believe I was running as fast as my superstar sister.

Matters of the Heart

When I got up to her and Pop, they were all smiles.

Denise gave me a hug and thanked me for helping her through the workout the way I had. "I couldn't have done it without you, Michael!"

I felt like king of the world at that, even though all I'd done was hold the watch.

Her cooldown was to take a mile on the track, and I ran the last lap with her. It felt like I was moving alongside the greatest runner of all time. And in my mind, she was just that.

As we jogged, we talked about the Phillies and she asked me what I was learning in school. The conversation didn't have a single thing to do with racing, just life, but it added to my running high. Or the running high I'd gotten off of her running.

When we finished, Pop handed Denise her sweatpants and told her to get them on so she wouldn't get sick. Then off we went back home, the three of us skipping as we did.

When Denise went up to her room to get ready for school, I asked Pop if he thought she could beat all those other fast girls she'd be racing in just a few short weeks.

He nodded. "I think so."

According to him, she was a dark horse: a competitor who might not be taken seriously at the get-go – but at everyone else's peril. Besides, "She has a look in her eyes," he added.

His tone was very serious, and I was just as solemnly paying attention to everything he said.

"Don't tell anyone, but I feel sorry for those other girls. Her times may not be as fast, but anyone can be beaten on any given day."

That last line might not have sounded so promising, but his next ones more than made up for it.

"Plus, she runs her best races in the big meets. She runs on heart. And you can't teach that; you either have it or you don't." He smiled. "If heart has anything to do with the winner, then your sister will do just fine."

I smiled back. I couldn't help myself.

"It's not necessarily the fastest in the race that wins, Michael," he summed up his larger answer. "Sometimes it's the biggest heart that does."

SEVEN

Racing in the Street

That weekend, Denise completely breezed through the regional championship race in Pennsylvania to qualify for the championship race in California. She had a week's time after that to go out to the West Coast, where she'd have to run one more 3,000-meter to qualify for the finals.

So out to California she headed.

It's only fitting that Patti was the one to escort her there. It just isn't an event unless Patti's involved. She's the one who makes a little gathering into a party in our family. Patti is hands-down the person you want in your entourage for any major event.

Certainly, she was up for this newest task. Years before mainstream cellphones ever hit the market, she stayed busy giving us updates from a payphone at a 7-11 down the street from the stadium. It was Patti at her best, protecting Denise as well as being a fountain of information for the rest of us.

That worked out perfectly for Denise, since she just likes to do the work and let someone else do the talking about it. Together, they made a dream team for a dream race.

Even so, it was impossible not to think about the odds when there were dozens of other finalists and families also California-dreaming that week. With the 50 best high school 3,000-meter female runners in the country assembled, two separate races would narrow down the fastest 16 for the finals. Those qualifying competitions each featured 25 girls trying to make the top eight in order to compete for the Junior Nationals crown.

As it turned out, Denise finished eighth in her qualifier. Her time going into the finals was about 30 seconds slower than the top seeds, which put her about half a lap behind the supposed champs. It also meant she was placed dead last in the finals for the women's 3,000-meter Junior Nationals Championship.

No matter to her though. She called home immediately to tell us the good news. By the grace of God, she'd made the final spot! She was, in fact, that dark horse my father had predicted she'd be. And that couldn't be better…

Because the one thing we all knew about Denise that no one else did was how she loved being the underdog.

As for me, none of those little details mattered one way or the other. I knew my sister would beat these other fast girls from places far from my house. On that, there was no doubt in my mind, at least not that day.

A Wing and a Prayer

The evening before the finals, I was looking at the map of the U.S. with Theresa while she explained how Denise was all the way on the other side of the country running against girls from all these other places.

"Do you think she'll win?" I asked, even though I couldn't actually imagine another outcome.

"If she gets a head start, she might," Theresa replied. "It isn't like all the races you've seen her run before though. This time, she's the slowest."

All of this, I understood. Technically.

"The girls in her race are the best of the best," Theresa added. "So first place? Just to finish in the top 10 would be a miracle."

The logical side of me knew she was right. Really. But when I thought about watching Denise run, I just couldn't imagine how anyone could possibly run faster. She was the type of runner who never showed weakness. Plus, she actually got faster as the race progressed. Like a boxer who won't go down and just keeps throwing punches.

Sitting there, I remember staring at the map and wondering if Denise was scared all the way on the other side of the country where she was.

That night, while Pop and Mom helped Marianne, Theresa and I say our prayers in the room we shared, we each prayed specifically for our far-away runner. Not that we needed the prompting, but Pop made sure to tell us she needed lots of prayers for her big race.

We could all tell he hated not being out there with her, but it just wasn't possible with his schedule.

A Chance Encounter

"Do you think she's got a chance to win, Daddy?" I asked as he was turning off the bedroom light.

"She's got a chance," he said in a soft voice. "She's got a chance."

That night, just to be on the safe side, I said an extra prayer to

God. Asking Him to help my sister do her best, I prayed that she wouldn't be scared – no matter how fast the other girls could run.

Marianne had told me the race was near Disneyland. So when I pictured it in my imagination, I saw Denise running right through the theme park. As I fell asleep, I had beautiful visions of her dashing down golden streets with Mickey Mouse and Goofy cheering her to the finish.

If anyone had a chance to win, it was Denise. Moreover, I knew that if she had a chance, she would somehow find a way to make it count.

Discoveries

I remember hearing the clock tick as my family sat together the day of the race. I even remember what I was staring at. It was the carved piece of wood Mom had above her kitchen sink that read:

> *Allow life's beauty to envelop you.*
> *Hold no guilt or worry about what should have been*
> *or what might be.*

I'd seen it a hundred times. A thousand even. I even knew its backstory... how one of Pop's Amish friends had carved out the black letters that now stood out so prominently.

Yet there's a major difference between seeing and reading. So of all the times I'd sat in our kitchen before, that day was the first time I ever read the plaque instead of treating it as just something above the sink that I ran by every day.

In all that quiet, I finally discovered it. And it seriously spoke to me in those moments of waiting.

My mom had a special knack for hanging appropriate sayings where they were obvious eyecatchers. So it made sense she would put such a sign above the sink, where she spent so many hours. Truly, God only knows how much time she spent at that kitchen spot.

Being a young boy, not to mention the 10th of 11 children, my focus was typically quite different in that family-oriented room. I was always in such a mad rush to get food that I rarely paid attention to anything but getting my seat before everything was gone.

Admittedly, the food would never be completely gone. But if you were late, you understood beforehand that your portion was going to be greatly reduced. It was an unspoken rule in the house. Just like in the jungle, it was survival of the fittest.

Or at least the most prompt.

Perspective

I can count on one hand how many times I've heard the clock ticking when everyone's together. We're just normally not quiet enough to hear it. Yet waiting for the news about Denise's race, everyone was feeling nervous enough to pipe down.

Other than our runner and Patti, of course, we were all sitting around the dinner table, each person in his or her "usual" chair. My spot was between Marianne and Theresa on a bench at the end of the table. It was also known as the "bleacher seats" in our house, a spot I'd been moved to right after graduating from my high chair.

On this particular day, that spot was allowing me to notice all sorts of hidden gems around me. This included another carving in the same style as the last, this one situated in the living room. It was another saying I knew existed but never bothered to actually read before.

Wherever you go, go with all your heart.

In fact, all around me, I realized, I was surrounded by pictures and sayings specifically created to lift the spirit. Working exactly how they should, they provided even an antsy little kid a source of peace and calm while I sat and thought about the challenges in front of Denise.

She may have been 3,000 miles away, running 3,000 meters against the rest of the country's best. But, once again, none of that mattered to me.

Even if she was the dark horse in her race, she was our horse. And that's all I cared about as I watched the slow hand make its way around our kitchen clock.

The Dark Horse

When Pop first labeled Denise as a "dark horse" in the national championships, I had to ask him what that meant.

"That's the horse no one thinks can win," he explained with a smile on his face. "Everyone except for the trainer and owner."

Hearing this, Marianne was quick to pipe in. "Does Denise have a trainer and owner who think she can win?"

"No doubt about it!" he responded.

"Who's her trainer?" I wanted to know.

Another smile. "That would be me."

"And her owner?"

"That would be God."

In my young mind, that seemed liked the perfect combination. It still does today.

Sitting there at the kitchen table that afternoon, most everyone there was old enough to know it was wishful thinking to believe she could do it. They knew she wasn't running against the best in the area. She was running against the best in the country – a big difference. So everyone really was trying to be realistic about their expectations.

Maybe she would have an incredible race and finish in the middle of the pack?

That would be good. Right?

For me though, I couldn't imagine a world where Denise didn't win such a monumental occasion. It just wasn't possible.

At 4:30, the clock was giving every indication that her race was over, since she'd been scheduled at the West Coast's one p.m. That meant it should be just a matter of a few more minutes before we'd hear the news. Whatever it was.

Denise had gone out to California on a long shot and a pair of legs with the impossible dream of not just running well, but winning the whole damn thing. It just wasn't in her nature to think about anything but winning it all, no matter how big the odds were stacked against her.

She was a true dark horse in every sense of the word for this race. And, like Bobby Bare once sang, "If you ain't got nothin', you ain't got nothin' to lose."

On that summer day, she didn't. Though that was no guarantee she wouldn't.

Pop started pacing the room as my mother and grandmother prayed the Rosary with their eyes shut – all in complete silence. Meanwhile, I sat quietly with the rest of my brothers and sisters.

Hoping.
Praying.
Dreaming for our Denise to bring home the gold.

Hearing the News

When the phone started ringing, there was a hush that came over the kitchen – something not often seen in my house. Linda went over to the phone and gave a look to the family, her reassuring smile helping to ease the anticipation.

When she picked up the phone, she was immediately greeted by a screaming Patti. From 3,000 miles away, our oldest sister filled us in on one of the best sporting accomplishments our family would ever experience.

Linda held up the phone as Patti kept yelling the news. "She won! You guys, SHE DID IT!"

The voice echoed through the entire house.

"She won! She won! Denise won the race!"

The house went even more silent with shock. Then everyone erupted, first with joy and then with tears. We went through so many powerful emotions at that announcement.

"I can't believe it!" I yelled at the top of my voice. "I cannot believe it!"

Marianne and Theresa were spinning me around, yelling, "She did it! She did it! She did it!"

It was pure pandemonium.

Somehow, someway, Denise had found a way to come in first. Legend has it that her finishing kick was so ferocious, she passed four people in the last 150 meters! And, legend or not, it was now an undisputed fact that Denise had beaten the best.

I will never forget the way I felt hugging my sisters and brothers in those moments after we got the news. The way I saw it, Denise could do anything. Absolutely and completely anything.

My sister was unstoppable!

"I knew she would win!" I kept yelling as I ran around the house, hugging everyone as I contradicted my initial outburst. "I knew it!"

It was an amazing feeling for everyone in the family to share. Our dark horse had won the race.

And like a true champion does, she and her bodyguard, Patti, celebrated her win at Disneyland.

SEVEN

A *Brady Bunch* Episode With a *Rocky* Storyline

A few days later, we all piled into two cars to pick Denise and Patti up from the Philadelphia airport. As expected, my family made a complete scene from the minute we walked into the airport until the minute we left.

This is something that used to embarrass me to death. Now it's something I've learned to use as another form of entertainment. I don't call it "making a scene" anymore. It's "family bonding."

As for that particular outing, Jimmy summed it up best when he said, "This is like a *Brady Bunch* episode with a *Rocky* storyline."

Jimmy usually is the one to sum things up best. He's a quiet observer who's able to assess a situation quickly and then turn around and summarize it in a few words or a sentence in a way the entire family can get onboard with.

Though had that week's events played out a couple decades later, he might have added another show to the mix. It was more like a *Soprano's* setting with a *Rocky* storyline and a *Brady Bunch* ending.

Just picture the whole family standing at the gate, waiting to go crazy and really make a scene the second Denise stepped out the door. The freak show was in full effect, and we were ready to explode with joy at the sight of our very own national champion.

Needless to say, we had some great "family bonding" when Denise came out the door.

Green Grapes

In typical Denise fashion, she was back to work the minute she got home. She didn't waste time even changing out of the running clothes she'd worn on the plane. She just put her bags down and started waiting on customers.

That day, we put up a big sign on the front of the produce market that said, "Congratulations, Denise!" And we kept it up for the remainder of the summer, partially because we were so proud and partially because customers would come up wanting to get a glimpse of her.

It was like having a minor celebrity on staff when she was working.

Even a grumpy old man we called Sour Grapes was happy about our champion. Then again, Denise had already made a mark on him through full force of her particular brand of determination.

He'd gotten his nickname in part based on how many times he'd come up and complain about everything under the sun, from gas prices to the hot weather. Though that alone didn't brand him as such. It was how he yelled at Theresa about getting a bad ear of corn the previous day.

"I'll take care of that guy the next time," Denise declared. "He looks like he just ate a sour grape every time he comes up here."

After that, the nickname stuck. So did her insistence that nobody else deal with him but her. So the next time he came to get fruit and vegetables from us, Denise took care of him. And the next time. And the next time.

And slowly but surely, Sour Grapes started complaining less and less.

Now, no customer was prouder of her gold than he was. He jumped out of his car and scurried up the driveway when he saw her working in her sweat suit just days after the race.

"I knew you could do it, champ!" he said as he approached her.

After that statement, Denise never called him Sour Grapes again. From that day on, he became known as Green Grapes, since those were his favorite.

The Wonder Years

Having nine older siblings has been great for many reasons, one of them being that I could – and still can – so easily pick and choose what I wish to learn.

All my brothers and sisters are so different. Yet we all manage to be interconnected. Coming from such a large family helped me to really see how who we are is influenced by others, and how others are influenced by who we are.

Growing up, Denise had a way of influencing me by her actions alone. She's a leader by example. Even with all the people coming and going in my house, I would always notice her doing her thing off in the distance.

Unobtrusive but oh-so powerful.

When the Time Is Right…

As her races often showed, Denise is patient with her moves and

SEVEN

her ability to prepare and wait for the right time to shift into higher gear. So it's no surprise how, when Pop found himself in the hospital all those years after her running days were over, it was Denise who set the pace for his comeback.

The family knew she was our lead runner in spirit still, and we all tucked in behind her.

Thinking back to when I watched her run those many moons ago, I can't help but recall how she would be so intentional about choosing the right time to pick up the pace. There was nothing formulaic about it.

They say that luck is no more than preparation and opportunity coming together at just the right time. Which means there comes a moment in every one of our lives where we must "make a move." And if we're properly prepared for it, then "luck" will surely be on our side.

That's what I learned from Denise both in running and again on that fateful Christmas morning in the hospital. In her own way, she's a constant reminder to be patient. Because the time will eventually come to make your move. It's not a matter of "if." It's a matter of "when."

So when it does, go with purpose and determination. And don't look back. Just open up your stride and dig deep into your heart on that backstretch even if the wind is in your face. It's that point when your angels are cheering the loudest for you.

It's also that point when God has your back the most.

Your job is to simply hit light and float at His speed – no matter the odds. Let Him worry about such things.

He likes that kind of stuff. Beating the odds. Taking the long shot. Backing the underdog. It's part of God's sense of humor, a way for Him to let us know He's still in control and that we're right where we need to be if we're only patient enough to wait on Him.

It's patience that wins the race when the odds are stacked against us.

When Pop was on what looked very much like the backstretch of life and the wind was at his face, Denise reminded him whose race he was really running.

You might not have a Denise in your own life, but the next time you're feeling the strain of the race, just remember to tuck in behind your angels and listen for Our Father's voice on the backstretch, saying, "You're right where you need to be!"

CHAPTER 6
Linda: The Rock

Peace

If I had a twin, I'm guessing that she would probably be a lot like Linda. In both looks and attitude, she and I are two peas in a pod. But in her case, she goes more than the extra mile. Our family's "Oprah," Linda inspires the troops and encourages our dreams. In battle, she's the one I'd choose to have next to me in the foxhole.

She's the personification of peace in a storm.

It therefore might seem like quite the contradiction to say she's also like a controlled tornado moving at the speed of sound. Yet anyone who knows her can see how both apply. She has this way of getting things done while still exuding restfulness, serenity, tranquility and quiet.

This amazing ability was on full display on Christmas Day 2011, and I know my dad felt it.

Like Marianne, Linda stands just a sliver over five feet, but she's not short. With her confidence and self-assurance, her physical vessel may be small but she is a mental giant. On a sports team, she'd be like a Cal Ripken Jr., in baseball or a Dick Butkus in football. In other words, Linda is in a league of her own: a true winner in what really matters in life.

She just gets it done any way it needs to get done. Plain and simple.

Going to the Chair

When I think of her, I think of a lifetime of great memories. That includes her role as the family barber, though I didn't recognize it as a great memory in the making at the time.

This wasn't something she was naturally suited for. Not in skill or in service. Yet family barber she was nonetheless.

Now that I think back, I suppose it's actually not surprising. She just has a way of getting involved wherever she sees a need. And since nobody else volunteered for the duty of salon-level stylist, she went for it.

I think Linda liked all the commotion around haircut nights, but they were an amateur's version of horror hour for me. Mom had to talk me into submitting to such non-tender care every time.

"It will only take a minute," she would tell me, her voice full of exasperation at my protests. "Just let her cut it!"

"No!" Oh, how I wanted to win those arguments. "She hurts my head and makes me look bad for at least a month. People laugh at me in school!"

"Well, your hair is just too long," she'd reply. "So you have to get it cut."

And that would be that. To the chair I would go.

I got a haircut twice a year, so maybe Mom was right and I should have simply sucked it up. But to me, that was two too many annual appointments with Linda as my barber. And should I ever have to take that chair again, I can't say I'd do it with any more grace.

Linda cut hair the same way she does everything else in life: with sheer determination! Which meant that, yes, it was an actually painful experience. This isn't to say that I bear any grudges against her for going through the task so fast. I don't. I'm sure that, had positions been reversed, I would have been the same way. With so many unpaid haircuts to give, time was of the essence.

Whenever a fateful Haircut Night came around, Mom would march us all onto the porch to sit on a bench. And wait. Just sit there waiting our turn. Waiting and thinking. And dreading.

Psychologists have long-since debated about which is worse: pain or the fear of it. But despite being subjected to both during those times, I cannot give an answer.

They were both bad.

It was torture knowing that, in a matter of minutes, Linda was going to chop off my curly black hair. Yet that didn't mean I was happy when those minutes were up. I was never happy when she got around to calling my name.

"Come on," she'd tell me while the previous victim, my brother Jimmy, shook the loose hair from his cut. "Get up on the chair."

Seeing his accidental mohawk would ultimately scare me enough to make one last attempt at getting out of it. "You know you don't have to cut my hair if you don't want to."

Not that she ever let me off the hook. It wouldn't matter how much I begged.

I remember how excited I was the first time I went to a real barber. Once I did, no offense to Linda, I started to love haircuts. I remember thinking, *I can actually look okay afterword!* As I remember, I did have a sense of guilt the first time I rode my bike up the street to see my new – and improved – barber, Frank.

Linda herself, however, seemed to take it well. With Linda, it wasn't a "barber-customer" relationship. It was a "person with clippers-test dummy" relationship.

Nothing personal whatsoever.

In a Field of Dreams

Of course, growing up with Linda wasn't all haircuts and horror. She was and still is one of the biggest cheerleaders I have in my life, constantly encouraging those around her and finding the silver lining in difficult situations.

She certainly encouraged me as a kid. When I was 11, Linda was the fuel behind one particularly memorable moment during my Little League days.

I'd been playing since I was seven, but this was the first time one of my teams had a chance to go to the playoffs. To get there, we had to play a team we were tied with.

The day of the game, I was so excited. I felt like I was getting ready for the seventh game of the World Series. The night before, I'd even slept in my uniform – and one that hadn't been washed in over two weeks. I had my shoes, glove, batting glove, bat and hat all next to my bed, ready to go, perhaps making me the most prepared participant in the history of Little League.

The only hitch in my mapped-out mental strategy was how I'd get to and from the game. That part, admittedly, was problematic.

It was the summer, so the produce business was going full steam. Worse yet, my game was at 4:00 in the afternoon, which was the busiest time of day for us. So there was going to be drama about me leaving. No ifs, ands or buts about it.

All in all, there were four factors stacked up against me:

1. It was a busy Saturday.

2. It was the heart of the day.

3. I was leaving "work" to go "play" baseball, something I knew my brothers would give me an earful about.

4. One of my older siblings would have to also leave work to take me.

I didn't say much during the morning or into the early afternoon, I wasn't looking forward to the moment when I would have to speak up.

When three rolled around, I was in my room, ready to go. I could already hear a little chatter in the kitchen, so I assumed it was about who had to take me. Only a moment later, I heard a knock.

It was Linda telling me to "get a move on it, 'cause the party bus is pulling out in five."

I sprung out of bed so fast my hat flew from my head. Grabbing up my stuff, I ran out of my room, marveling at how there had been no drama after all like I'd so expected. Linda just took the bull by the horns.

Since there were so many of us siblings out and about, having one-on-one time was precious. Usually, you had to talk over three or four people when you tried having a two-person conversation; so it was nice not to have to shout when we got in the car.

I started thanking her, but she immediately stopped me.

"Don't thank me, Mikey," she declared. "You just got me out of work!"

We talked and joked the whole way to the field. And before I could walk off to join my team and she could walk off to sit in the stands, I told her I'd get a hit for her.

That made her laugh. "What about a stolen base?"

I promised her two.

The Last Thing to Die

The game didn't start out exactly as planned for my team and me. For that matter, even going into the last inning, we'd only managed to scrape out two runs. Otherwise, we were getting our hats handed to us. The score was 5-2, and I hadn't kept any of my promises to Linda.

I had no hits and no stolen bases.

Yet I will never forget my coach's speech right before that last inning. Mr. Constantine was ready to take a bunch of scrappers and lead us to victory, and he had no problem showing it.

"Hey, guys. Listen up!" He demanded. "We still have a chance here. We got three outs and a lot of hope! And, gentlemen, hope is the last thing to die."

With that, the Twadell Plumbing team absolutely exploded. Mr. Constantine's speech got the whole team fired up. Our first few guys got on base and we were right back in the game. By the time I came to the plate, we had two outs and the tie run on second.

I didn't know it right away, but I was about to have my greatest baseball moment ever.

Stealing Home

Bing!

The 2-2 pitch flew off my bat and into the gap in right center, prompting me to fly forward as fast I could.

I rounded first. Then second. And I could hear Mr. Constantine yelling, "Turn three! Turn three!"

So I flew headfirst into third, taking that as well.

We had officially tied the game!

My team was going crazy while I jumped up from my slide and threw my arms into the air in triumph. Nor were they the only ones enjoying the show. When I looked over at Linda, she was dancing around with the other parents, just as exuberant as they were.

SEVEN

Calling a timeout, Mr. Constantine came over and put his hands on my shoulders as I was trying to dust off all the dirt on my shirt from the headfirst slide. Then he looked me right in the eyes.

"You know what you have to do," he said. "Right?"

I knew exactly what he was saying. We'd already discussed before the game how the other team's pitcher was lazy on the mound. He was a big kid with a rocket for an arm, but he was slow, seeming to just take his time in a cocky sort of way.

That didn't mean my heart wasn't pounding furiously as I watched that big kid throw the first pitch. It was low and in the dirt, but the catcher blocked it.

My coach and I both knew that stealing home was a long shot. But it was our best shot at the moment. To steal home, I would have to time it perfectly on my break for home plate. If the catcher saw me too far off third base, he could pick me off.

This was dangerous territory, to say the least.

As the catcher threw the ball back to the pitcher, I put my head down. And ran.

I could hear the other team's coach yelling, "He's stealing home! Throw it! Throw it home!" Above and around him, the crowd erupted as I raced toward the plate for the final play of the game. The umpire's call would determine which team was going to the playoffs and which team's season was over.

I kept running.

The pitcher caught the ball and whizzed it back to the catcher. And still I kept running.

The ball hit the catcher's mitt just as I dove headfirst into home. My hand slapped the plate to the almost instantaneous declaration of "Safe!"

That meant I'd done it. We'd done it! We were going to the playoffs! My team rushed out of the dugout to hoist me onto their shoulders, adding to the moment.

But the best was yet to come after the game when I reunited with my big sister.

"Mikey, I knew you were gonna score the game winner," she exclaimed with a huge smile on her face as we drove to the Lickity Split Ice Cream Shop for a post-game celebration. "I just knew it in my heart!"

She was so excited for me, and that right there meant the world. I'd played the game just like she would have... all out, with my foot on the accelerator.

It's hard to top that feeling.

The Fan Favorite

Linda is a star no matter what she does. She shines so bright and helps others do the same.

She might not have been as fast as Denise, but Linda was a track star in her own right. The stadium would just come alive during her races. She was pure energy on race day – what horse racers would call a work horse and what one of her coaches called a fan favorite. Both are Linda in a nutshell even to this day.

Although I could tell you all about the races she won, the one that sums her up best is the one she lost right at the tape. That was the 3,200-meter county championship her senior year, after which Pop couldn't help but declare how, "People pull for Linda the way they used to pull for Seabiscuit."

Sure enough, the crowd was pulling for her so much that, when the race ended without her taking the title, the entire stadium was affected.

Linda really did all the work that entire race. The whole time, she set the pace and blocked the strong winds blowing that day for the pack of runners behind her. So when the girl who ran behind her for every step of eight laps took her on the final step, the whole stadium let out a gasp.

It wasn't a loud cheer like you'd usually hear at the end of such a close race. It was a great big, "Awww!" And then there was complete silence while Linda lay on the track like a prize fighter knocked out by a left hook to the chin.

In the end, it didn't matter what place Linda finished in. It was more that, when she ran, she had a look of complete determination on her face and in her style. While Denise floated around the track, Linda powered around it like a freight train.

Leave the Gun, Take the Cannoli

My favorite Linda running story is when she was in high school. She and Denise went to different high schools, and they were scheduled to run against each other in the two-mile.

This race was a very big deal in my family for two reasons. One, because they'd be in the same race. And two, because Pop was bringing Nu-nu, our grandfather, to his first track meet. It was the first time my grandfather had come to see his granddaughters run, and Pop wanted to make it as exciting as possible.

Since Denise could probably lap Linda if they really raced, he put in "the fix." It was set at dinner the night before, when everyone was weighing in with their opinion on how the race needed to go.

In the end, it was Pop who set the plan – just like the mafia fixed the Jake LaMotta and Sugar Ray Robinson bouts, except I doubt they did it over hot apple crisp with Breyers vanilla ice cream.

The rest of the family agreed that a tie was a must if Nu-Nu was going to be there. Denise's coach wanted her to run a different kind of race, we knew, but she decided to listen to Pop instead.

"The Fix"

So there Pop was, fixing the race. And there both of my sisters were, fully committed to the fixing.

The day in question dawned beautifully; it was a perfect spring afternoon. The birds were chirping cheerfully as I sat in between my grandfather and father, listening to him ask question after excited question while my sisters warmed up on the infield.

He was like a little kid as he watched his two granddaughters take their positions. And when the gun went off, it ramped up his excitement even more.

"There-ah they-ah go!" he exclaimed.

The field of girls ran as a pack through much of the first mile, exactly according to plan. But after that, Denise and Linda slowly started to pull ahead.

Nu-nu, usually a reserved man who rarely said a word, was on his feet cheering them as they slowly increased the distance between them and third place.

Coming through the sixth lap, Denise was running easy as Linda plugged along with her. Since we were up on a hill around the 100-meter mark, we could see everything perfectly. Yet we were still close enough to hear the clanking spikes on the bottom of their racing shoes and the sound of the runners' breathing as they passed by. Being such a perfect spot, most of the assembled students and parents were also sitting on this hill, and they really started to come alive as my sisters clipped off the laps.

It was a beautiful sight to see them pulling each other along around the track.

Thatta Was a Race!

As they entered the final lap, everyone around us was standing to watch this wonderful race happening before them. Two sisters. Side by side. The whole way.

Pop, Nu-nu and the rest of the family were yelling to them as they ran by us, stride for stride around the track to come across the line, tied for first.

"Now thatta was a race!" Nu-Nu declared. "Are dey all like-ah dat?"

"They're usually even more exciting!" Pop replied with a big grin.

Even to this day, when he talks about his favorite races, this one stays in a league of its own. He loved watching his girls, and he loved watching Nu-nu watch them.

My grandfather made no secret about how much he enjoyed the event. He talked about it to everyone and anyone who would listen afterward. Being such a quiet guy overall, it was out of his character to talk too much about anything. Yet he kept saying in Italian, "It was like watching a ballet!"

The Big Race

Not long after that race he was taking care of his tomato plants and the other vegetables he was getting ready for the summer. It was an unusually hot day outside, but that kind of thing never stopped him from tending his crop.

All morning, he'd talked about the race and how he couldn't wait to watch Denise and Linda run in the state championship. But while he was working, he had a heart attack.

Mom was standing across the lawn when he fell, and she rushed to his side, performing CPR on him and everything. It just wasn't enough though. Only two weeks after watching his first "ballet" on the track, he was gone.

The man who had brought the Marini name to the United States of America in 1921 had finished his own race. Apparently, he'd already had his clothes laid out in anticipation of Denise and Linda's next event, despite it being so many days away.

SEVEN

He was that prepared – almost as if he knew he was getting ready for something enormous, complete with a destination we all hope to go to someday. Denise and Linda got to play a part in that, no matter how unexpectedly. And that's a beautiful thing.

Meeting the Family

Growing up, I didn't need TV. I had enough entertainment watching all the different boyfriends float through the house.

It was entertaining in the extreme, and I loved when a new one was coming over. Pop and I would just sit and watch TV while whichever sister ran around trying to get ready for the evening.

I would usually hear them yelling about someone being in the bathroom too long while they frantically tried to get ready before the date arrived. The longer it took them to get ready, the more time Pops and I had with their prospective suitor.

Most of the time, the guys who came to the house were completely overwhelmed. Understandably so. And I did feel sorry for quite a few of them. It's bad enough having to go visit anyone's family for the first time, much less a family like mine.

Personally, I liked to stare them down a little to see how they'd react. Most of the boyfriends were nice enough to me, though some of them weren't so nice to my sisters. I could write a whole other book on what I've learned from them alone.

If I did, it would be called *Go With Your Gut*. I say this because the ones who turned out to be good guys, I liked in the first 10 seconds. The ones who turned out to be jerks, I disliked in the first five.

Pop used to label the jerks as "bozos." He would sometimes joke at dinner on a Friday night, "Hope we don't get too many bozos coming through the house tonight."

Some of my sisters encountered more than one "bozo" along the way, but I never had to worry about Linda's love life. She met her husband-to-be at a track meet in eighth grade and immediately came home declaring, "I'm going to marry him."

She went on to date him through high school and college, and sure enough, they eventually married and had three daughters.

He was one of the first boyfriends I remember meeting, and I liked him right off the bat. So I did like any six-year-old boy would do if he met one of his sister's boyfriends that he liked.

To the shock of my family – and certainly to him – I punched him right square where it counted.

Big Picture

When it comes to most things, Linda just seems to "get it."

She's the kind of person who can relate to anyone on any level – except maybe when it comes to haircutting. That's probably why she turned out to be such an incredible nurse.

Linda knows what's important in life, never seeming to lose sight of the big picture no matter how crazy things get around her.

Like our father, she laughs at herself a lot. Also like him, she stays the course. She's steady and strong.

In short, Linda is a rock.

Give Peace a Chance

Although I've seen a lot of ups and downs being in the large family I'm in, Linda is the one who's probably shown me the most ups.

She gives great advice and peace of mind to the point where it bears repeating that she really is the rock in the family. She always has been, though it wasn't until I saw her with my father in the hospital that I truly realized the peace she radiates. It's her natural state of being as she takes care of business and stays true to the course.

When I meet a strong and confident woman, I think to myself, "They have a little bit of Linda in them."

Linda has always told me to go for it. She's supported my talents in life, teaching me to stretch those doubles into triples in Little League and beyond… Teaching me to get people fired up!

Passion is contagious, and Linda both knows it and shows it. She has what it takes, and she's very well aware of how to spread it to those around her – a fact that stood out so strongly that Christmas morning with Pop. Linda took control of the storm, showing how priceless it is to have peace in your spirit.

She just goes to show how, no matter what storm you're in, you can make it through if you let God be your captain and peace be your sail.

CHAPTER 7
Kathleen: The Heart of Seven

Grace

While Kate – Kathleen – and I were moving Pop's bed so he could be near the sunlight, I saw a look in her eyes. It was a look of complete determination. She knew my other sisters were doing their things, and she was doing hers. As usual for Kate, she gracefully did her job with no fanfare.

Kate is what we call a "behind the scenes" type of person. She doesn't like the spotlight, and she just proceeds on course – her course – never letting the little stuff distract her. Growing up, if there were any fights or arguments in the house, as there inevitably were, she would be the last to jump in.

Kate just minds her own business in an almost humble way, yet she's usually the first to jump in if anyone ever needs anything. In her own unique way, she just has a way of getting through any problem or hurdle she comes across in life.

That Christmas Day, I think Kate spoke the least out of everyone in the room. But she got the most done. After we moved the bed, she made sure Pop was in the exact spot she wanted him. And that precise placement, complete with the care and love put into it, did wonders for our father.

Then, after we moved the bed, she worked as auxiliary support to each of my sisters in whatever task they were doing. Typical Kate, amplifying everyone around her as she so naturally does.

Roll With the Punches

When we were growing up, mornings were the most chaotic time of day in my house. Alarms would be going off, there'd be fights for the two bathrooms that six of my sisters and two of my brothers shared, and then there was the usual hunt for breakfast.

Everyone would be running around trying to figure out travel plans for getting to school. There were also lunch discussions to be had, rides home to be sorted, afterschool plans to be determined... And, like most Italian households, there were also inevitably discussions about dinner as soon as the day got underway.

All plans were sure to change five to 10 times if one of my sisters was involved.

I've already admitted how I was usually the last to rise. That was largely to miss the early-morning circus (and partially just because I wasn't a morning person). But Kate was even better about staying out of all the commotion than I was.

She just did it by getting up first and quietly going about her routine.

In so many other ways, I did my best to follow Kate's lead in that regard. Being the youngest for the first seven years of my life, I learned early on to not ask many questions and just roll with the punches.

Every Day's Game Day

Every morning, the house had that "big game" feel to it. Some days, if enough big events were happening, you could feel a buzz running through the house like a bolt of lightning.

It was just like the feel inside a baseball stadium as the pitcher gets ready to throw the first pitch. Or the energy radiating from a football stadium just seconds before the kicker sends the opening kick into flight. The same electricity you feel seconds before the Kentucky Derby announcer yells those famous words, "And they're off!"

Maybe someone would have a big exam or a big sporting event

that day. Maybe one of my sisters had a crush on a boy and was extra excited because she was going to see him soon. Or maybe it was just the general excitement of what every new day could bring our way.

But odds were, with the number of kids in the house, someone would have something big going on that day. And whatever it was, Kate would usually be the one to tell it to the family. She was and still is the family announcer.

Before there were cell phones to pass along big news about major events, Kate would keep us all informed of the family highlights.

The Fundamentals

Another big part of our mornings was Pop and his quotes. It was like having Vince Lombardi, Jim Valvano, Tony Robbins and Yogi Berra all wrapped in one and sitting at our kitchen table. In a lot of ways, this added to the day's big game feel, with his inspirational quotes sounding like a coach motivating his players in the locker room before they take the field.

My father would rattle off one quote after another while all of us scrambled to get something to eat, grab our lunch and race off to catch the bus or our ride. It would be an absolute zoo, with everyone running around getting ready for the day. Yet there he would sit, delivering one saying after another like he was reading them straight from a book.

"You only live once. But if you do it right, once is enough."

It was his way of getting us ready for the day ahead and the work that needed to be done. Life can get hectic around us, but it's the fundamentals that keep us grounded and drive us on.

"Just keep your eyes on the fundamentals" was another one of his favorite parting pearls of wisdom as we ran out the door, the fundamentals being all the things that make us who we are and set us on our path in life – everything we are at our core. In my house, they were simple: Work hard and stay the course until the job is complete.

Since the house was like a three-ring circus, it makes sense that the simple things were stressed the most.

Yet another one of my father's favorite lines was, "There's a price to be paid for success. That price MUST be paid in advance."

It was a maxim that Kate especially took to heart. Just as she was usually the first one up in the morning, she was also the first one out the door as a general rule. She kept to herself, stayed out of the commotion, got her work done – and kept her eyes on the fundamentals.

In general, when my father spoke, it was Kate who heard him the most. Without saying so many words, she had a way of setting the tone. Unlike some of my other sisters, who did their fair share of talking, Kate just let her actions convey her thoughts.

Bring Your Own Container

One thing was absolute at my house each year… When the leaves started to fall, we knew the Christmas business season was fast approaching. It was kind of like that annoying uncle or aunt you have to see every year for certain holidays.

It wasn't that we didn't enjoy it per se, just that we knew the workload that came with it. That workload was intense.

Yet whether we enjoyed it or not, the business would roll in each year like a freight train onto our property. We would have rows of Christmas trees lined up in our driveway, and we did all the preparations in the garage.

Every year, it went the same way. To get everyone prepared, Pop would have his annual pre-season meeting at the kitchen table. He'd post a sign in the kitchen that read "Come to the Meeting – Free Knowledge. Bring Your Own Container" complete with time and date.

Most of the time, he'd add a quote underneath it, choosing something depending on the family's mood. "TEAM – Together Everyone Accomplishes More" was one of his go-tos when it came to rallying the troops for the grueling season ahead. Everyone had to carry their own weight; otherwise it made for an even longer stretch. So we each did our part, from oldest to youngest, including my mom's mother who we called "Mom-mom."

The word "enthusiasm" comes from a Greek word that means "God in you." And when it came to getting everyone pumped up for the end-of-year chaos that the Christmas business inevitably presented, my parents needed a lot of God in them to get us ready.

We all did.

My mother would usually start the meeting by serving a nice

SEVEN

dessert. Then Pop would stand at the head of the table and thank everyone for being there with, "I know you're all very busy, so I appreciate you coming out tonight."

From there, he'd run the meeting like any other CEO. Except that he was the CEO of employees who were very outspoken and hard to please. Also, we weren't in any fancy boardroom with suits and dresses. It was all 13 of us around the kitchen table in our pajamas.

In that informal setting, complaints were inevitable.

Someone might complain about their pay or argue about what food should be served at lunch on the busy weekends. Or any number of other irritations or concerns. We went through it every year.

Each year, there are rumors that it's going to be the last. But after five decades, it still hasn't happened. So no matter how the meeting might end and who swore they weren't working or who'd flat-out get up and leave, Pop would end on a positive note. "Well, let's try to have our best year yet. I know we can do it!"

It was kind of like *Groundhog Day*.

Studio 2121

There were many nights growing up that my brothers, sisters, and I worked past midnight for the Christmas business. Personally, I enjoyed working late at night with my family, though it did lead to some interesting memories.

Since I was the youngest working in the garage for a while there, I'd be in charge of getting drinks if anyone was thirsty. My father would yell, "Who wants hot chocolate?" and then get a count. "Okay, Michael, can you please go tell your mother we need eight hot chocolates and six iced teas?"

I loved going inside and waiting for Mom to prepare all the drinks so I could take them back out into the December night. Watching my family work in general was really quite a sight. Pop would be in his glory, rattling off poems and quotes if he ever saw the mood change.

Which it inevitably would.

Multiple times.

With so many siblings and so much work, it was practically a recipe for fighting. Frustrations would mount, and someone would usually end up blowing their lid.

It's Not Work; It's Cross-Training

Whenever those arguments broke out, Pop would stand back and let it go for a little before trying to ease the tension with his version of a funny joke. "You know, some people would call this work. But I think they should call it cross-training."

This was one of his favorite late-night lines. Clearly, he was no Johnny Carson, and he rarely got any laughs – not even from Kate. But when the work was done, we'd still all talk about the particular quotes he delivered that night.

The truth was that all 11 of his children working away into the wee hours of the night made him proud of the business. It wasn't just work he'd started to help put food on the table. Nope. It was our family business that we all contributed to.

Just like Santa's workshop, we would come together to get ready for the big day.

As for me, for the first 13 years of my life, one of my biggest jobs was to keep the garage warm. This meant I was in charge of the pot-belly stove. Out of my countless tasks and responsibilities as a kid, this was by far one of my favorites. I felt that maintaining a comfortable temperature for everyone there was something my brothers and sisters relied on me for.

Believe it or not, I especially enjoyed going into the field and chopping wood. No one had to tell me to do it. I was on top of the situation, monitoring how much or how little wood we had without a single prompt from anyone else.

If I saw the supply getting low, I'd just let everyone know I was going to get more.

Late at night, I'd bring a flashlight to place on top of one of the famous Amish-made wagons I'd tow along. The wood was kept in a field behind our house, which was always a peaceful place at such late hours. Even so, my sisters would make a big deal about it since it was typically so cold out.

"Bundle up, Michael! It's freezing out there tonight," Denise would yell.

"Don't let any coyotes get you," Linda would usually joke.

Then there was Kate, who would be quietly working in her station, decorating wreathes. Whenever she'd see me getting ready to get wood, she would stop and offer to help.

"I got it, Kate," I'd tell her. "I can handle it."

"Oh, I know you can, Mikey," would be her inevitable response. "But four hands are better than two. Plus, I just want to get some fresh air."

Sometimes, she'd subside after another assurance from me. But the times she did come along – they stand out. Kate had a way of making me feel like I was doing the toughest job in the world, bragging to everyone how well I could chop after we came dragging the full wagon back.

Even at that young age, I knew she was doing it out of love, not because she was thrilled to go out into the cold December night. Yet it was a bonding experience, and we more than managed to make it fun as a general rule.

The two of us would load up the little portable radio on the wagon and listen to the classic rock station as we loaded wood, talking music and dissecting songs. Kate was the professor of music in my eyes. She knew all sorts of interesting facts about different singers and groups, providing what felt like an entire encyclopedia's worth of knowledge on the subject. So I soaked up every fact she fed me.

There was also always a sense of anticipation whenever Kate would go out with me to chop wood. Everyone knew it could only mean one thing. The dancing was going to begin soon. For that experience alone, I'd happily keep that pot-belly stove going all night for my family.

"Funkytown"

Before the late-night arguments would commence, my family operated like clockwork when we all worked together. But as the night progressed, it was mildly entertaining to watch everyone get delirious from too much work. Linda would lose it first, then Joey, and on down the line.

Some nights, admittedly, we needed to blow off steam more than others. And Kate would be the one to show us how to do it: line dancing to '70s tunes.

Whenever she told us to get up, we listened, putting our work away for 15 minutes to let her lead us through the incredible licks of "Funkytown" or whatever else our self-made DJ decided we needed. It was really fun for all of us, and we got a lot of laughs out of it – especially at Pop's expense.

One of the highlights of the night would be watching him dance. He does this one move we call the "Shake It Out," which consists of shaking his wrists like he's warming up for a race. That only makes sense, I suppose, when he's famous for advising, "Just shake it out," along with his vast collection of other sayings.

He wasn't the only one who got to show off his dance moves though. Thanks to Kate, we all had a chance to practice our skills. Joey would be doing his "breaking in the house" dance while Danny did the "sprinkler." Meanwhile, Jimmy and Marianne would perform the "shopping cart" as Linda did "the robot."

With so much work to be done for the business, it was typically hard to stop and play. But those breaks, short though they were, were extremely effective. Once we got back to work, the mood would be completely different and we'd get what my dad called our second wind.

Whatever it was, we had Kate to thank for that boost of pure energy on nights that otherwise took their toll. With her around, there was no quitting until the job was done.

Father and Daughter

Out of everyone in the family, only one followed Pop into his exact field. Although my three brothers work in agriculture, Kate is the only one to have the same job.

I'm sure if my father had to pick one of his children to follow so closely in his footsteps, he wouldn't have orchestrated it any other way. That's because it's so simple. If you give a project to Kate, two things will happen:

1. It WILL get done on time.
2. It WILL get done right.

Kate is like clockwork. Whether in her daily life or on the job, she makes it happen. While I can't help but feel a certain sense of laziness compared to any of my sisters, Kate is by far the worst in this regard. Seeing what she can do in her 24-hour days compared to what I do in mine makes me sometimes wonder if I'm getting less time.

SEVEN

She'll accomplish a Michael's week's worth in one single Kate-infused day. She really can do the work of about three people on her own.

Quality Time

It was the summer of 1990, and I was only a month away from beginning high school. Kate was working in Colorado and I was out visiting her, giving us the chance to cruise along I-70 in her Jeep Cherokee with my favorite Cat Steven's song, "Father and Son," playing on the tape deck.

That's when I got to gaze at the Rocky Mountains for the first time, and what a sight it was! Well worth the trip all by itself. Though, of course, the landscape wasn't "all by itself." There was also Kate.

Usually, I would have been up with Patti in New York City for my summer vacation, but she was too busy that year with her new nursing job. So it was Kate who I reached out to next, and she responded by promptly inviting me to fly out to her house and travel Colorado, Nebraska, Wyoming and South Dakota with her. It would be a true bonding experience and a trip that had a lasting impression on how I saw her.

She took me under her wing for two weeks and introduced me to some of the most beautiful areas in the Land of the Free while simultaneously showing me another world of music. The way I see it, Patti introduced me to Bruce Springsteen, Linda introduced me to Genesis, and Kate introduced me to everyone else.

That trip also had a lasting impression on how I saw myself and the many possibilities life has to offer. I can remember turning to her at one point to say, "Someday, when I grow up, I'm going to live near the mountains." Sure enough, a decade later, I was living in Colorado to take in those consistently amazing views.

I wouldn't have gotten to watch the sunset behind the mountains so many times if it wasn't for Kate. She may not have known it at the time, but that trip would plant a dream in my mind.

Amazing Grace

They say that 80% of success is just showing up.

Well, Kate shows up 100% of the time and typically gives even more when it comes to effort. Never making a lot of noise but always doing her job – that's how she operates.

Joey and I sometimes joke about how much our sisters are overachievers. And, for the most part, they are.

Not with Kate though. She's not an overachiever; she just does a whole heck of a lot.

Very driven, you can bet she'll be committed to this project or that. And while she may be one of the busiest people in the family, she's by far the most organized. If she says to be there at noon, that means not a minute after.

Kate is the very model of timeliness and precision. She's reliable in all the best ways. Reliable and determined. But there's more to her than that.

If you look up the *Oxford Dictionary* definition of the word "grace," you'll find the following description: "simple elegance or refinement of movement." And that is so true of Kate. She takes resolve to a whole new level and makes it look lovely as she does.

You know that look in someone's eyes when he or she is on a mission? With Kate, that look was never surprising, and I saw it once again when she was directing my father's bed into a visibly brighter spot.

The fear of failure – or of anything else – cannot stop a brave spirit. A humble, persevering spirit will beat the odds every time, since it's drawn to the light by the grace of God.

CHAPTER 8
Marianne: The Dream Painter

Faith

"When Uncle Tubi was your age, he was supporting his family."
I seemed to hear that Uncle Tubi line every time I complained about working too much at our family businesses. In all my years though, I never once heard Marianne get told that, probably because I never heard her complain about working too much.

An employer's dream machine, she works hard, keeps her mouth shut, sees jobs that need to be done and does them without being told. Watching her, I used to think she was the female version of Uncle Tubi since she was always working so hard at whatever she did.

Legend has it that Uncle Tubi really was supporting his family by age 11. It's almost funny how we remember him, I think because each of us feels a touch of him in our blood. Each of us has a little bit of that family-line workaholic trait. It's just simple genetics when you get right down to it.

And those genetics stand out strong in Marianne.

Many of my siblings refer to Pop as the workhorse of the family, but he refers to Marianne as such. She's a throwback to the old days with her "old-school" way of life and work ethic.

Marianne doesn't like to beat around the bush. She likes to know exactly what's going on, and then she wants to deal with it. And she'll tell it like she sees it.

Hard Times

I was in third grade, and it was the winter of 1984-85, the heart of the '80s. Reagan was at the height of his presidency, and there seemed to be a sense of innocence in the air for most of the country.

For my family though, it was a rough time. We were recovering from another grueling Christmas business season, and one that hadn't paid off. Out of all the years in that decade, this one sticks out the most.

It was a brutally cold December, and it rained on two of our most crucial weekends – times we should have sold a majority of our trees. Between the two environmental factors keeping people indoors, we had almost half our trees left by the 20th. At that point, we just loaded up the trucks and drove around town, giving them away to people.

Of course, this is the risk any business takes. But that wasn't our norm, particularly for all the effort we put in.

On top of that non-norm was the much more common "winter blues." At least that's what I called it whenever the business finished up and everyone went their own way again. So much energy and focus went into the Christmas season that, when it was over, we basically had to pick up where we left off two months earlier.

That required a certain adjustment period, which could be rough, particularly when so much of our family together time came to such a halt. Add that up with the frustrations of all our hard work seeming like it was for nothing, and it was far too easy to get some serious blues that time around.

Eye of the Tiger

Despite the winter blues, Marianne and Theresa got right back into their routine of running and exercising after school every day.

SEVEN

For my part, it never occurred to me to run with them. That was their thing. When it came to sports at the time, all I cared about was baseball.

So when Marianne asked me to come running with them one day, I had a very quick answer.

"No way! It's cold out, and I'm not in shape to be running with you guys."

"Oh, come on," she replied. "It'll help you with baseball."

That's all she had to say to grab my interest. I asked a few important questions about the pace and distance I'd have to run, she answered them, and we were out the door.

Little did I know I was on my first vision quest, with Marianne leading the way.

For the rest of the winter and into the spring, I tagged along with those two sisters of mine. Our routine was simple: Go to school, come home, run, do our exercising, do our stretching, eat dinner, do homework, watch TV, go to bed.

For the first month, it was hell almost every day. I cried daily because I was so frustrated with my sisters and with myself. Since they were in better shape than me, they'd be running at least 50 yards ahead, making me downright angry inside. After all, they'd told me, their younger non-running brother, to come along. They should wait up!

But they didn't.

Instead, about a month in, they decided to take me on my first "long run." We were riding home on the bus that particular day when Marianne turned to me.

"So, are you ready to run five miles today?"

Considering my track record up 'til then, I'm not sure why I replied so confidently. "Yeah, I'm ready for sure!" Yet she took me at my word.

For whatever reason, we headed out a little later than usual that afternoon, and the cold was intense. My sisters made me bundle up in six layers of clothing to protect against the elements, which was fine with me.

I used to wear a towel around my neck whenever we ran. I had seen a picture of Rocky Marciano, my favorite boxer, wearing a towel around his neck when he was training and I decided to follow his lead. Though, unlike him, I would keep my hood up so that no one could see my face. The way I saw it, I was in secret training. Complaints and righteous indignation aside, I wanted to have the mindset of a contender getting ready in the wilderness for the shot at a title fight.

Lost in the Garden of Arden

Unfortunately, on that go-round, the extra clothing backfired a bit. Once we got about two miles into the run, I started to get very tired with all that extra weight on me.

"Come on, Michael!" Marianne yelled as we ran through the little town of Arden. "We're not even halfway there yet!"

But I just couldn't keep up no matter how hard I tried. My sisters kept pulling ahead while the sun began to set on that bitter-cold Delaware day. I was still about two miles from the house when I lost them altogether.

I stopped to catch my breath outside the Arden Theatre, sitting on a bench and trying to think of a game plan. But with the wind kicking up a bit, it was hard to focus on anything more than my potentially impending doom.

It didn't take long before I began to cry.

I was all alone and scared. The bitter cold was burning my lungs, and I felt like I was carrying a piano on my back.

Once I got my breath back, I started to run the rest of the way home, my fear fueling my once-tired legs. It actually felt like I was floating as my feet barely hit the ground, and I could feel my stride open up further as I dropped my arms to use them more. With each step, I could feel the ground moving beneath me, taking me one bit closer to home.

And every bit closer I got, the fear was melting away to make room for wonder. Very slowly, mind you, but receding nonetheless.

Sprinting down Sunset Court, I saw Mr. Pallini, the nice Italian man whose house was in the field behind us.

"Hey, Marini! What are you doing out here in the dark?" he yelled at me.

I yelled back as I ran by. "I got lost on my run, but I'm okay now!"

It was the first time I saw just how fast I could really move if I put my mind to it.

That didn't mean I didn't start crying again when I got home. While a part of me stayed excited about how fast and far I'd run, another part stayed scared about being alone like that.

Of all people, I expected Marianne to have pity on me for my predicament. Normally, she would be the first to console me if I was upset. Yet she didn't this time. She wasn't even close to sympathetic, and I'm glad for it now.

"You need to start keeping up with us," she informed me. "I know you can."

She was right; and in that moment, I knew it. As such, it was the last time I complained. After that, I kept my mouth shut and just followed them until I got in better shape.

By the end of the winter, I was running side by side with my sisters.

Dreamweaver

Every new day that came, we could see our progress, which was awesome. And Pop got in on the act too, leaving us little workouts to do Mondays, Wednesdays and Fridays.

Tuesdays and Thursdays, meanwhile, we would run on feel. That basically meant that, however we felt that day, we'd go with it. If we felt good, we'd run fast. If we were tired, we'd do a light jog.

Those were nice, but there was something compelling – even motivational – about the workouts Pop developed for us. On those days, we'd get off the bus and run into the house to see what instructions he'd have.

My father is a true genius when it comes to running. What he says about the sport has always been like gold to Marianne, Theresa and me. So when he told us repeatedly that, "Every time you train, it's like putting money in the bank. You cash it at the end of the season," we took him at his word.

With that mantra ringing in our ears, we thought about how exactly we'd cash in all our hard work. And, in typical Marianne style, she had a clear vision of our goal.

"What if we all won the half-mile at the CYO Championships?" This was the Catholic Youth Organization's final meet or, as Marianne told us, "the only one that matters. All the other meets are just warmups."

Theresa and I thought it sounded great. For all of us to win would be such an amazing accomplishment. The only problem was that, for the final meet, they only let sixth, seventh and eighth-graders run. Since I was in third grade, that meant an automatic non-qualification.

But Marianne didn't care about such technicalities. According to her, it wouldn't be a problem. She'd talk to the coach and have him enter me with the sixth-grade boys.

"No way!" I initially protested. "I'm not running against sixth-graders! They'd probably lap me, and its only two times around the track."

Marianne would hear none of it though. "Mikey, I think you can win! Just think, no one would know who you were. You'd be the dark horse of the race. The underdog. Just like Rocky."

She had my attention after that. She knew how to direct my determination just like she had when prompting me into running in the first place.

I was completely sold, and so was Theresa. From that day on, we trained with one thing in mind. We were going for it!

With that goal established, Marianne next taught me about the concept of visualization. "Just picture the whole race," she said. "Visualize yourself running it from the gun until you cross the tape."

So that's what I did. Every night, before I went to sleep, I'd visualize myself running in that championship event. I could see the whole thing from start to finish. Almost like it had already happened, and I was simply remembering it.

As it turned out, Marianne had taught me one of the most valuable tools I would ever use in life.

The Breakfast Club

I remember hearing the birds chirping outside my window – and Danny's radio on full blast – as I woke up on race day. Somewhere inside me, I guess I had hoped the day would be a rainout, thus sparing me the potential humiliation.

It didn't rain though. Not even close. It was a beautiful Sunday morning.

From a strictly environmental standpoint, May 21 had arrived in the most beautiful of fashions possible, wrapped in sunshine with singing birds. From a strictly emotional standpoint, the atmosphere felt heavy. All those days of thinking and training were about to come to a head.

SEVEN

The pressure was on. In more ways than one.

The family was still pretty revved up from the high school state championship the previous day, where Danny had competed in the 3,200-meter championship race.

Maybe he was still feeling a little too good about finishing his high school career on such a strong note. Maybe he was just in a mood. At any rate, the morning of my race, he was up early and blasting Phil Collins' "In the Air Tonight." And since his room was right next to the one Marianne, Theresa and I shared, we could all hear him loud and clear as he kept singing the same line over and over.

"I've been waiting for this moment all my life!"

Jimmy, who shared a room with him, was begging him to stop while I dragged myself out of bed. Clearly, Jimmy didn't appreciate it. But for this day's three contestants, it made for a light morning. Which we really needed.

We were nervous wrecks.

As with most mornings in our house growing up, the kitchen was the most entertaining room in the house. It was the closest thing we had to a Marini stand-up comedy club.

As we ate our pancakes, Danny distracted us more with his brand of humor, joking about his race the day before. "Yeah, I thought there was still another lap to go when everyone started sprinting down the homestretch."

Joey was quick to respond to that one. "You never were very good at math, so that makes sense." The two of them were like Dean Martin and Frank Sinatra when they got rolling, with Joey being the clear "leader of the pack."

Danny kept rattling off one joke after another, and Joey would add in a zinger after each one.

Marianne, Theresa and I hung on their every word the whole time. It was Danny and Joey at their best, and at just the right time too.

Dream to Catch

After breakfast but before the race, we were sitting in church as a family and I was reflecting back on the past four months and how far I'd come.

It gave me such a feeling of peace looking at it that way. Even though I hadn't run in a single other race that season, I realized I should be proud for getting to the point I had – particularly when I didn't even like track at the time.

So why go for it exactly? All I knew was I had a dream to catch. I wasn't thinking. I wasn't analyzing. I was just doing. And the fact that this wasn't my sport made me even more of an underdog, which I liked. Just like Denise, I suppose.

Plus, I really, really loved the picture Marianne had painted for me. It got me pumped up whenever she told me I was the real-life Rocky. That sounded awesome.

Truly though, everything Marianne said to me stuck. If she told me I could do it, then I could most definitely do it.

At the church service's sign of peace, where we were directed to greet each other, Marianne leaned in to hug me. "Today is the day. I know you can do it."

That made me even more proud of myself and – miraculously – not guilty about it at all like I usually would. Growing up, I typically interpreted the command to be humble as a call to not feel good about one's achievements. Which could be quite the heavy burden for anyone, child or adult.

Except for that morning. That morning, I was ready to revel in what God had given me and I had utilized. The sign of peace had brought the exact comfort it's supposed to. It had done its job and then some.

The nerves wouldn't kick in again until after church.

Nobody's Fault but Mine

I was the clear-cut underdog in that race through full fault of my own. Marianne might have prompted me into it, but I had accepted that prompting. Though, in my defense, there wasn't too much wiggle-room to get out of it after she started bragging about my chances.

Two days before the race, my third-grade teacher, Mrs. Gricol, had told me she wanted to see me at the end of class. Naturally then, I thought I was in trouble.

"I hear you have a big race this weekend?" She smiled, regarding me from behind her glasses.

Mrs. Gricol was a runner herself who would often participate in various road races, and I liked discussing the topic with her.

SEVEN

Actually, I liked talking to her about anything. She was my second-biggest crush of all time.

Even so, I tried to play it cool. "Yeah, you know. They told me I'm scheduled to run on Sunday. It's not a big deal though. My sisters dragged me into this whole thing."

I was leaning on her desk, almost in a flirty fashion. An outsider may have thought I was hitting on her. And maybe I was in my oh-so suave third-grader fashion.

"I'm not really thinking much about it though," I added with the same sort of self-important dismissal. "Baseball is my sport. I just run because my sisters told me to, so I'm just happy my baseball game is on Saturday. I'd hate to miss it for running."

But Mrs. Gricol would have none of it. "Forget about that baseball stuff right now. You have a big race to win on Sunday! I was talking to Marianne in the hall after lunch, and she thinks you can do it. She sounded pretty sure about it too."

"Oh, that's just Marianne," I insisted. "It's my first time running such a long race, so I'll just be happy not to come in last."

I don't even think she was listening as I tried to talk myself out of winning. She was too busy writing something down on a piece of paper.

When she was done, she handed it to me. "Now go win your race. On Monday, you can tell the class how you beat out kids twice your size."

A GIANT Story in the Bible

I didn't look at the note until I got on the bus; but when I did, it was pretty powerful. On the one side, it read:

> *1 Samuel 17, David fights Goliath.*

And the back added:

> *Look this up and read it before your big race Sunday.*
> *He was a little guy with a heart of gold just like you.*

Her advice prompted me to actually read the Bible on my own, which was definitely a first in my life. At church, the morning of the race, I pulled out the piece of paper she'd given me, feeling like

I was glowing as I read about little David beating the giant.

A lot seemed to sink in as I did, hitting home as it only can for an underdog facing his own fight. I knew I'd be just like David in only a few more hours. Except my Goliath was a group of sixth-grade boys.

When church was over, we got in the car and headed to the big race, with none of us saying a word. All of us knew we had a big afternoon ahead of us, starting with me. I was scheduled to run first in the boys' sixth-grade 800-meter championship. Theresa would run shortly after me, and then Marianne would be the grand finale on the Marini agenda.

The track awaited.

Something to Believe In

Standing in the bull pen moments before the start of my race, I'll admit I was having some major doubts. Although it was great thinking about the possibility of winning that morning, once I saw the people I was running against, my shot at greatness just seemed out of the question.

"I'll be lucky not to come in last," I protested to Marianne. "I mean, look at them. I come up to their waist!"

I was throwing every excuse in the book at her, but she wasn't fazed. "Size doesn't matter. You've done the training, Mikey. Just think about all the training you've done to get here!"

"No way." I was adamant. "I want to go home. This is stupid. I don't even like track."

I may have been feeling frantic at that point, and I was definitely mad at her for dragging me into such a mess. "I'm a baseball player. You and Theresa are the ones who run track!"

So she switched away from logic to more psychological tactics. "Listen, Mikey. If you want to leave you can," she told me.

I did.

"But I think it would be a big mistake." She was nothing short of certain as she spoke. "Just get in there and do your best. Forget about everything and just run."

I could feel something shift inside me to head in a bit more of a positive direction.

The starter was yelling as her words sank in. "Sixth-grade boys, half-mile, please step onto the track."

SEVEN

One way or the other, it was time to face the music.

Marianne practically walked me to the starting line, whispering in my ear as she did. "You're the dark horse. No one even knows you. So have fun out there!" She smiled. "You can even wave to the crowd if you want."

We kept walking. One foot in front of the other.

"People pull for the underdog; and in this race, that's you!" she said.

With those words, she somehow made me believe. She's always had that effect on me, but that particular time really stands out.

Marianne is the only one who could have talked me into running in this race. With anyone else at my side, I would have chickened out. Easily.

One Foot in Front of the Other

Bang!

The gun fired, and off we went. Most of the sixth-graders in the race really were twice my size. Some were big for their age, whereas I was very small for mine at the time. In fact, I was the second smallest kid in my class that year.

It therefore wasn't surprising when, immediately, I was pushed to the back of the pack. And for the record, I stayed there for the first 200 meters.

Once we hit the homestretch of the first lap though, I started moving up. Twelfth place quickly became eighth as I passed kids twice my size. The crowd came alive watching me, and I fed off the energy of the cheering spectators at Baynard Stadium.

Coming through the first lap of that 800-meter race, I passed one more boy, putting me in solid seventh while I set my eyes on the top three. I was hardly in the worst position anymore. Not by far. So that was something.

Now officially entering the bell lap, or final lap, I remember Marianne and Pop cheering for me. Really, the whole place was loud and chaotic, but that was something I was plenty used to. So it actually calmed me to some degree. In another sense, I felt utterly electrified as we came through the halfway mark.

I was in fifth place as I passed Theresa, who was standing on the backstretch.

"You have 200 meters left!" she shouted. "Kick now. Kick now!"

Her words raced through my ears and through my nervous system.

"Go, Mikey! Go now!"

I took her advice and put on the kick of my life. The next thing I knew, I was in second place, with the leader right in front of me and 100 meters remaining.

The crowd was cheering so loudly, but the only voice I could make out was Marianne's as she screamed, "Get on your toes! Get on your toes!"

It was complete pandemonium as the leader and I raced neck and neck down the last 50 meters of the homestretch. But like I'd done all winter and spring, I listened to Marianne. I got on my toes and cashed in everything I'd put in the bank, closing my eyes and wishing for the finish line with every ounce of energy I had.

With a final lean, the race was over. I knew I'd crossed the line, but everything else seemed hazy. I really wasn't sure what happened until I heard my sister's voice.

Interlude Into a Dream

"Michael, you did it!" Despite being right up against me now, Marianne was still screaming, she was so excited. "You did it!"

I was in a daze, wondering if it was really over. For some reason, it all seemed like a dream as Marianne supported me off the track while the other runners were still finishing.

"What happened?" I asked. "Where am I?"

"You were awesome!" was her response. "You out-leaned the guy right at the end. You did it! You won!"

I was still trying to catch my breath, feeling like I might literally die if I didn't get it under control. It was the fastest I'd ever run, and what a time to do it! But my hands were now on my knees, and I just wanted to take in the sweet spring air.

"Keep walking," Marianne coached. "Just keep walking. I can't believe what you just did. You ran it perfectly!"

Oxygen was slowly returning to my lungs. And my brain.

"You were amazing!" my sister kept gushing. "Just listen to the crowd! Those cheers are for you, Mikey!"

I have to admit it did feel amazing as I walked off the track, arm in arm with her to the cheering grandstand.

"Give them a wave. They love you!" she told me as I worked so hard to put my one foot in front of the other.

I looked up to see if I could find Mom, but my sight was still blurry and I just couldn't locate her. Marianne could see I was still out of it, so she told me to go lie down on the infield while she went to pep-talk the next Marini contestant into her race.

It was Theresa's turn now, and she was apparently a nervous wreck.

Still Can't Write It Any Better

I thought I was bad before my race. But Theresa was apparently 10 times worse. By the time I crossed the finish line, she'd already thrown up twice behind the concession stand.

Marianne certainly had her work cut out trying to keep her calm until she got to the line. Theresa looked like a skittish race horse before the bell. She was all legs and bucking wild as Marianne tried to get her in the gates.

But Marianne knew it was just a matter of getting her to stay calm until the gun. And, sure enough, once that went off, there was no question who was going to win. Theresa took off like a bat out of hell and continued to pull away the entire time. Nobody else had a prayer.

Once she crossed, capturing the championship, it was all on Marianne. The completion of our dream was entirely in her lap.

From a purely visual standpoint, she looked a lot like I had in my race. All the other girls just towered over her. Not that it had mattered with me. And it certainly wasn't going to matter with her.

Of that, I was sure.

It was only fitting that our goal of a successful triple threat should come down to Marianne. She was the one who first mentioned it, so she could complete it. Which is precisely what she did, flying across the finish line in first place.

I felt so proud of us that day, standing on the infield to collect our medals. It was a very special moment for me: the first time I had thought about something that intently and made it happen that amazingly.

The whole thing had me fascinated! I thought I'd learned a cool new trick, and I was determined to try it again. As I did though, I realized it wasn't a trick but a way of life.

It was a great day for the whole family, and Pop especially was just beaming with joy. "You guys were incredible!" he told us. "You could not have written it better if you tried."

Once again, my father was right. All these years later, and I still couldn't write it better. No matter how hard I tried.

Interlude out of a Dream

I remember never wanting that day to end. It was like Christmas on steroids, and the sun seemed to be shining 10 times brighter.

After we got home, we went to play in the field behind my house: the same spot my sisters and I had trained on for the last four months. We didn't play baseball or kickball; we "played" running, setting up relay races with Marianne, Theresa and I against Danny, Jimmy and Kate. There was so much laughter and lightness that followed.

Eventually, of course, the day ended as days are prone to do, and we all headed to bed. Sharing a room with Marianne and Theresa all those years, we'd had countless bunkbed talks before, but that night stuck out to a significant degree. So excited about what we'd accomplished, we all agreed that we wanted to be state champions together too.

We were now going to set the groundwork for our next vision quest.

The Pneumonia Story

There I was, a junior in high school, sitting in my pediatrician's waiting room with a two-year-old and a five-year-old, the patients after me. The only magazines to read were copies of *Highlights*, so I picked one up to take my mind off the situation. I'd already had X-rays taken and was now just counting down the seconds until I knew the results.

I'd been sick for a couple of weeks by then, and Mom had finally dragged me to Dr. Borin's office to get checked out.

It had been a while since I'd been to the doctor's, so I was still going to the same one I'd seen since being born and apparently would continue to see through college. He was normally in a great mood, so it was an automatic bad sign when he looked as severe as he did after calling Mom and I back in.

"Michael, the X-rays we took of your lungs are not good. You

SEVEN

have pneumonia."

That didn't sound healthy.

"It's a wonder you've been able to run the past couple weeks," he said with a shake of his head. "Looks like you've had this for a bit now, and your running is making it so much worse. All that needs to stop now, and we need to just focus on getting you better."

That really didn't sound good. Or acceptable.

"Good thing your mother brought you in today or you could have done some serious damage," Dr. Borin declared, his words and tone and dramatically moving hands all emphasizing his diagnosis. "Your mother tells me you still want to run this season. Is this true?"

Now he sat back in his chair and crossed his arms, another sure sign he meant business.

However, so did I. So I straightened up in my seat. "Absolutely. There's no way I'm going to miss the states in May. I've been training all year for this race."

In case he'd missed my point, I added, "It's my race. It's my year."

Perhaps I was being a little dramatic myself.

"Nothing is going to stop me from getting in that race!"

Make that a definite to being dramatic.

Dr. Borin one-upped me though, slamming his hand onto the big oak desk. "Now, Michael, you listen to me and you listen good! You are not running for at least three months. And when you start running again, it can only be jogging. Running in your little state fair race in May is not happening!"

I was anything but persuaded.

"You're not comprehending the magnitude of this illness," he continued. "I'm the doctor, and you're the patient. And now is the time for you to listen to me."

I could tell he was fired up. I could also tell he knew he wasn't getting through to me. So he raised his voice a little more, which was an attention-grabbing decision in and of itself. Even with his traditional good humor, Dr. Borin was a proper man who normally spoke with a certain eloquence.

I used to think he sounded like the Rockefellers, even though I'd technically never heard one before.

"When is this race of which you speak, Mr. Michael Marini?"

I cleared my throat. "May 22."

That resulted in a decidedly less-than-eloquent response.

"Are you out of your mind, young man?" He turned to Mom. "Mrs. Marini, put this one to bed for a couple weeks. He's not thinking straight with his fever. Which is 102, by the way!"

Turning back to me, he was hardly done yet. "Your state fair race is in five weeks? You have pneumonia, Michael! Do you know what pneumonia is?"

There was no room given for me to reply.

"It's fluid in your lungs! Running in races and pneumonia do not mix. It is crazy" – he put a special emphasis on that word – "to even think you can run in a race in five weeks! It is simply out of the question."

He seized onto another line of reasoning. "You're only a junior. You still have another year. It will be fine."

I shook my head though. "I'm still going to try and run. It's not the state fair; it's the state championship. And even if I get lapped, I'm running in that race."

With this, he looked at Mom again. "Is this one adopted, Mrs. Marini? He doesn't listen like your other children."

Determined that I would be made to listen, somehow, someway, he asked his nurse to get my coach's number so he could call him on the phone and tell him that my season was done.

"There will be other seasons and other races," he explained. "You just have to let this one go."

Lost Cause

Driving home, I stared out the window of Mom's car. It was a perfect spring day with fluffy clouds, blue skies and the smell of hope in the air.

Hope that apparently wasn't for me.

I was devastated with the news that I had pneumonia. It boggled my mind to think I wouldn't have an opportunity to run in the state championships I'd been training so hard to participate in the past year.

All the times I got up before school to run.

All my afternoon practices with the team.

All the cardio I did at night riding the stationary bike and lifting weights.

SEVEN

Yet just like that, the season was a wash. All the training and dreaming had just been rendered futile.

I truly did feel as if a dream had died, and on such a perfect day too. I'd envisioned myself finishing in the top three in the two-mile. At times, I even thought that, if I got lucky enough and the race went my way, I could actually win it. It was a dream I'd wanted to reach since that night eight years before back when Marianne, Theresa and I talked about it.

No one knew I wanted this more than Marianne, who was now three weeks away from graduating college. Watching her win the two-mile two times at states back when she was in high school had been inspiring. Seeing her reach her dream had given me that much more fire to reach my own. And I really thought I'd get the chance in May to do exactly that.

But now it was gone.

Even if I was in complete health – which clearly, I wasn't – I would have only had an outside chance of winning up against so many top-notch athletes. But being sick made my odds fly right out the car window while we drove down the street heading to our house.

Mom tried to console me, but I was a lost cause. To me, it seemed like the end of the world.

It wasn't something I got over in a day or two either. For the next two weeks, I did a lot of soul-searching. This included reading Norman Vincent Peale's *The Power of Positive Thinking*. If you ever need a shot of quick inspiration, read the first chapter of this book. It's called, "Believe in Yourself."

And believe me, it helps!

The Dream Painter

Not being able to run was hard. So every night after dinner, I'd go for a walk on the track across the street.

I was doing a lot of visualization at the time, a practice I'd already gotten a lot of use out of ever since Marianne first told me about it. And it was Marianne again who would actively remind me about the importance of "seeing myself get better."

Since I've made a habit of listening to her, those words made perfect sense to me – at least on one level. My body would simply have to follow my mind. Whatever I could dream, my body would do.

Well, every night as I walked around that track, I dreamed of winning the 3,200-meter State Championship. Since I had fluid in my lungs from the pneumonia, it was hard to run anything, much less almost two miles. I'd get these awful cramps anytime I tried that were 10 times worse than a normal side stitch.

As such, my visions were the only things keeping me going at the time. Yet even so, and as much as I trusted my sister, I wasn't sure if my dreams were realistic considering my circumstances.

What I didn't know quite yet was how everything would change once I went to see her graduate from college.

Setting the Stage

I can remember daydreaming about running as we sped down I-95 South to North Carolina, with Danny averaging 85 mph the entire way. That factor wasn't surprising. Danny only drove one way: fast and furious, just like he did most other things in life.

As such, I didn't talk to him too much. That way, I wouldn't distract him or increase our chances of dying in a fiery wreck.

The family was on its way to our seventh college graduation, this one at East Carolina University, where Theresa was also enrolled and I would one day receive my own degree.

We made it down in one piece — thank the Lord — and proceeded to swing into the typical party weekend we were used to expecting from Marini graduations. This included a gathering at Marianne and Theresa's place, which was right off the Tar River in a small two-bedroom apartment they shared with a brother and sister.

The brother, Ronnie, loved Phil Collins. Like really loved him. According to my ECU sisters, it was the only music he ever played.

Naturally then, he played "In the Air Tonight" four times in a row at the party – the same song Danny had belted out the morning of my third-grade race so very long ago.

At one point during the party, Marianne pulled me aside to see how I was doing. "That really stinks your season is over," she commiserated. "It must be killing you."

As usual, she completely understood. She's one of the greatest listeners in the world, a fact that can melt away a whole lot of resistance.

Before that moment, I'd refused to talk about being sick with anyone. My whole family knew what was going on, of course, though not because I told them. It was the typical Marini tabloid that announced it. We had our very own weekly gossip line, and I knew my story had been front page news since the Dr. Borin visit.

Now, to Marianne and only Marianne, I opened up. "Well, I can't run, but I have been doing a lot of that visualization stuff you taught me."

I told her how I'd been envisioning myself winning States, and how it felt like it was real. How there were only two major barriers keeping me from solidifying that vision.

One was the fact that I couldn't run more than 500 meters without having to stop.

The second was that I technically wasn't in the race at all.

The Michelangelo of Visions

I had only run one two-mile race that year back at a dual meet in late March. It was raining and my third race of the day, so my time wasn't great. I was ranked 18th in the state as a result, and in the state championships, they only line up the top 16.

After I explained all that to Marianne, she took control. "You should do it, Michael." She shook her head in amazement at just the thought. "Wow, that would make for such a great story."

I swear, when it comes to motivational efforts, that girl is better than Tony Robbins. With those words, she awoke a sleeping giant in me.

Marianne had a knack for saying things in a way that just seemed to make sense. And on this day, she got me so excited that, within 10 minutes of talking to her, I was ready to sprint out the door and run 100 miles.

Emotionally speaking.

Physically, of course, I was hardly healed. But she set up the entire dream for me anyway.

"Daddy already told me he thinks you can do it," she explained. "He thinks it's a vision quest. I wouldn't tell too many other people about what you're thinking, but keep that vision in your mind regardless."

Although my father and I had never spoken the words out loud, we both were thinking the same thing about me running in the championship on May 22. After watching the movie *Vision Quest* just a few days after my visit to Dr. Borin's, he'd started randomly reciting the final scene's big speech at the end of meals. Everyone would laugh because he was paraphrasing it and adding in his own lines.

I'd known he was thinking something big, but hearing it from Marianne solidified my thoughts about having a vision quest.

She spoke with confidence, as if it was already a done deal. "If two people decide not to run the two-mile, you'll be in the top 16. Just have faith, and the rest will take care of itself."

With her laying it down so easily, it didn't sound even close to impossible. I was hanging on her every word.

"Then, all you have to do is go down to the state meet as the two-mile's dark horse. No one will have any idea you're there until they line you up for the start."

I could tell she was getting more and more excited herself.

"Michael, this could be the greatest comeback of all time. It's better than *Rocky*!"

As she painted that picture for me, I could hear Phil Collins in the background, singing, "I've been waiting for this moment all my life."

An Outside Chance

Marianne knew Pop and I had been watching clips from the *Rocky* movies every night before I went to bed. She also knew it was the missing element that would sell the dream.

And it did.

At that moment, as we stood on her back porch, I decided there was nothing else in the world I wanted to do more than toe the line for the state championships. Just like that, hope came alive in my spirit and I could enjoy the beautiful Carolina spring night.

I knew I had no control over the situation. But if two people decided not to run, I'd at least get a chance. So there was a chance I'd get my chance.

Since contestants are only allowed to run three events at states, they don't necessarily run every event they've qualified for. They don't necessarily even want to. The 3,200-meter, after all, is a long race. Why run it if you can prove yourself elsewhere?

That would be some people's thinking, at least. Perhaps even enough for me to qualify.

The more I thought about it, the more it seemed possible.

Calm Before the Storm

For the next two weeks, I spent a lot of time thinking, praying, visualizing, walking and meditating. And Marianne was around for all of it. Since she was done with school, she had some time to relax – time she used to bolster me.

Having her around gave me strength every day. No matter what doubts popped into my heart or mind, Marianne would erase them simply by her words. And so the day of the "dream" kept approaching.

My father would say that character is what you do when no one is watching except God. So I spent all my alone time building my spirit to face an impossible task.

Believe it or not, the days leading up to the race were very relaxed for me. By then, I felt fully guided by my sister's encouraging words.

My father was also a great support during this time. He and Marianne were the only two people in the family who knew I was even considering running. Everyone else thought I'd resigned to the fact that my season was over.

Yet Pop would tell me stories every night about people who'd beat the odds. He talked a lot about Roger Bannister, the first man to break four minutes in the mile. And he was sick the entire week before he broke it.

Aided by those true tales, Marianne's quiet confidence and the meditation I was doing, my mind was overall quiet and focused. I knew I was in no physical shape to run two miles. But in my heart, I thought about nothing else but winning the whole damn thing.

In the Air Tonight

Two nights before the race, I walked into the kitchen to get some water, only to see my father and Marianne having an intense conversation at the table. Pop was holding a piece of paper in his hand.

"You may want to come take a look at this, Michael," he said. "The final list came out today."

I knew he was referring to the official list of runners. It's announced two days before the race who will be competing in each event, along with their seed times.

Sure enough, Pop continued while I walked over. "It looks like your sister was right. Three people dropped from the two-mile. Take a look at the 15th seed."

As I looked at the list, my heart jumped with both fear and excitement. There my name was, listed in black and white. I had made the cut and would be seeded 15th out of 16 runners for the state title.

Which was scheduled to be run in 48 hours.

"Holy cow. I made the list." I tried to sound confident, but I was actually terrified now that this first part of the dream was becoming a reality.

Marianne could hear the fear in my voice, so she said something to pump me up a bit. "You know, we've been talking and we both think you have a chance in this thing."

I honestly wasn't sure if she was serious, so I jokingly said, "What. A chance to get lapped?"

Yet she looked me straight in the eyes. "No, we think you could win it. You're a complete dark horse. No one knows where you've been all season."

She certainly didn't sound like she was teasing.

"You know how it goes in the big races," she went on. "It's tactical, and the pace is sometimes slow at the beginning. If you can stay in it and make one big move toward the end, maybe you can steal the whole thing! No one's going to be looking for you after all."

She and Pop went down the list of runners, detailing why each one didn't have the heart to take it out fast or really go for it. And at the end of the analysis, Marianne picked right back up.

"This race isn't going to go to the fastest runner. It's going to go to the one with the most heart, and that's why you have a chance. The fact that you're even thinking about running it shows you're already a champion."

Wow, but she was good.

"After Saturday's race, you will never be the same. This is your chance, and we both really do think you can do it."

My vision quest had, it seemed, grown somewhat murky since that conversation we'd had back at her graduation party. I hadn't realized it until now. Yet she took her powerful paintbrush and touched it up in all the right places to make it stand out clearly all over again.

As such, half an hour after finding out I was in the race, I made the announcement to the rest of my family. I was officially in.

It was front-page Marini news.

Lying in bed the next night, my mind wasn't racing like it normally would be before such a big event. It was calm, and I felt a feeling of peace in the air. The waiting, the dreaming, the worrying was about to end very soon.

Believe

While the night was a peaceful one, I was a ball of nervous energy the next morning. Perhaps my sisters expected that. At least they'd certainly been proactive while I slept.

When I got up to take a shower, I was greeted by nine different signs on the way to the bathroom alone.

"Go Michael!"

"BELIEVE"

"GO FOR IT"

"YOU'RE THE CHAMP!"

My favorite was the one that said, "TODAY IS THE DAY!"

Marianne, Theresa and Angela had made them all for me, decorating the basement, where my room was located, and my bathroom as well. It was one of the sweetest things anyone had ever done for me. The nerves remained, but I can't say how much that show of support meant anyway.

After I showered, I went upstairs to be immediately greeted by Marianne, who gave me a big hug. "Today is the big day. How do you feel?"

"To be honest," I responded, "I don't know what I was thinking doing all this."

But she was right there to breathe life into my spirit again. "I'm going to take you down to the meet. You can get there an hour before your race and just start warming up immediately. That way, you won't have to sit in the sun or see anyone. You can just go down there and run."

Apparently, she and Pop had discussed it before I came upstairs. That plan had never occurred to me, but it sounded like a marvelous idea now. I calmed down quite a bit with that course of action before me, even sitting down to eat a peanut butter and banana sandwich with Linda and my oldest niece, Lindsey, who was just a year old at the time.

She had brought her over to calm my nerves before I headed to the stadium. In true Linda fashion, she brought my spirit some much-needed peace the day of the race.

Pop and Marianne also sat down to eat with me, making light conversation that helped soothe my nerves further still.

Lucky Charms

For the car ride to the race, I was surrounded by my gang the whole way there. Marianne was our driver that trip, with Theresa as her copilot, and Angela and I in the backseat.

Theresa was DJ and made sure to play Led Zeppelin's "The Rain Song" three times to set the right tone for the events ahead. She knew it was the song I'd been listening to while visualizing the race for the past five weeks, as it just so happened to be only one minute shorter than the race itself.

Other than that, the ride was pretty quiet for the most part. Though I do distinctly remember Marianne telling the story about the day she won states herself. Being a two-time, two-mile state champion herself, she had plenty of expertise to offer on the challenge I'd set in front of me that evening.

I loved to hear her and Theresa brag about themselves a little bit, no matter the reason. Marianne usually isn't one to talk about herself like that, and I knew full well that the only reason she was doing it now was to help calm me down. Again. Now that we were actually on our way, the gravity of what I was about to face was sinking in and the pre-race jitters arrived in force.

It was five o'clock when we arrived at the stadium – one hour 'til race-time. "It's time to do what you came here to do," Marianne told me as I stepped out of the car by myself to start my warm-up run and stretching routine. Then she went to go find a parking spot, leaving me standing there, staring at the back of our family's

SEVEN

black Honda Accord.

All on my own now, everything was quiet like I was in an orb. I couldn't hear Marianne's stories or Theresa and Angela's laughter anymore. And so I made my mind go completely silent as well. Silent except for Marianne's parting words.

It's time to do what you came here to do.

They were so simple, but they had such a huge impact on me.

Perhaps the universe knew I could use additional "huge impacts" though, since Linda pulled up alongside me before I could make my feet move.

"Hey, Mikey! Ready for the big day?" she yelled out the window.

"Yeah, I guess so," I responded.

"I have your good luck charm in the back!" She said with a huge smile on her face.

Lindsey was sitting in her car seat giggling and playing with her stuffed bear as the Genesis song "Ripples" blasted from the minivan speakers. As I opened the minivan door to give Lindsey a kiss on the forehead, it made me laugh how Linda was listening to her "pump-up song" on my race day.

Babies, when they're not crying of course, can be such a calming presence: a comforting impact even for the most skittish of dark horses.

"I can't wait to watch you run!" Linda told me as I closed the door again.

And so I headed for my warm-up run in the wooded area behind the stadium, thinking how things were really just clicking so far that day. Phil Collins' "In the Air Tonight" played through my headset as I jogged, something I'd been listening to a lot lately. It had become a sort of theme song the last couple weeks, with Pop even requesting it after Marianne's graduation party.

"Play that 'I've been waiting for this moment all my life' song," he said one night as he was walking past my bedroom. "I like the drums."

The Bullpen

For the big meets, like the state championships, the next runners up are put in the bull pen. Usually, you're only in there for as long as the prior race takes, but those vary greatly. If it's the sprints, you may only have to wait a minute or two. With the two-mile, you may have to wait 20.

My plan was to enter the stadium only after I heard the final call for my race over the loudspeaker. But that still meant I was stuck in the bull pen for far too long. The race before mine was the girls' 3,200-meter. And it took a while to finish. A couple of the participants got lapped, and it took them some time to clear the track.

As anyone who knows anything about preparing for a big event – particularly a sporting event – will tell you, waiting one minute, much less more, is the worst.

While in the bullpen, I had to stand with all my competitors, with this being the first time I was seeing most of them at all, since I'd been sick most of the season. I'd been nervous and scared enough before I got into the stadium. Now, standing with my rivals who'd been working so hard and so long to get where they were, it was 10 times worse.

So many thoughts went through my head about the race. In the back of my mind, I knew finishing at all was going to be a struggle. And that depressed me to no end. I didn't want to get lapped, much less have to drop out altogether. Yet there I was, putting myself in a ridiculous position where either could very, very easily happen.

Where either probably would happen.

Just as I started to really psych myself out, I felt a tap on my shoulder. It was Marianne, and in her hand was a small item attached to a safety pin.

It was a Blessed Mother medal that Mom had gotten when she was in Italy.

"Here, Mikey." She handed it over to me. "Pin this to your shirt. I forgot to give it to you before you got out of the car."

Accepting it from her outstretched hand was a very big deal. I knew that medal had been worn by my sisters and brothers before this moment, each one for their own biggest races. It was the first time it was ever handed to me though, and I felt like a knight being entrusted with the Holy Grail.

This was a sacred moment, one I felt right down to my core.

Pinning the medal onto my shirt right above my heart, I gave Marianne a high five and walked out onto the track behind my competition.

It felt like she'd put wings on my back.

SEVEN

Champions Enter the Ring Last

Marianne and Pop had set a game plan for me that was sheer genius, and they overlooked no detail in the process – right down to when I should step out onto the track.

"In boxing, the champion always enters the ring last," Pop said with assurance. "Remember that as you are stepping on the track. It's the way champions arrive for a fight."

So that's what I did. I let all my competitors step up first, making me the last to enter the battleground. As my foot hit the track, it was like pure electricity running up through my legs and out my fingers. I felt light glowing around my head, feeding further off the electricity of the stadium.

Phil Collins might not have been playing in my ear anymore, but he was still playing in my head. Something big was about to happen.

I can feel it coming in the air tonight.

The moment of truth had arrived, yet I felt a spirit of peace inside me come alive, channeling the coursing electricity in all the right ways. Every mile I had ever run in my life had prepared me for this race. I really had been waiting for this moment all my life.

The Race

"Runners, take your marks!"

Like everyone else, I was already there though. Standing in the eighth lane, almost off the track, I realized what a true dark horse I really was.

The starter pointed the gun in the air.

I took a deep breath.

Bang! The starter shot his gun, and so began the boys' 3,200-meter state championship race.

Looking back, my memories seem like a dream. A very vivid dream, but a dream nonetheless. I can remember how hard I was breathing in the first lap. I can remember Pop standing in his usual spot, all by himself at the top of the backstretch. And I can remember how, when I ran past him after the first lap, already dead-last and definitely oxygen deprived, he yelled, "You're right where you need to be!"

I laughed in my head at that, thinking that if dead-last was where

I needed to be, then I was in big trouble. Yet I can also remember saying over and over in my mind, *I'm in God's hands. I'm in God's hands.*

When I went by Marianne, Theresa, Linda, Denise and Angela, who were all standing at the 200-meter mark, they were kind of quiet. Even Marianne sounded nervous as she yelled, "Just be patient, Michael. Let the field pull you along."

So I did, trying to keep contact with the lead group with each passing lap. As we ran past the mile mark, I had moved from 16th place up to eighth.

Each time I went by where my sisters were standing, I could only make out what Marianne was saying. The other four were politely clapping and probably a little nervous for me, but Marianne seemed to have worked out her own nerves. She was in the race with me now, and I could hear it in her voice. Her tone gave me faith and hope that I actually had a chance, and her words wiped away any lingering doubts I had of getting lapped. They put me in the reality of the situation.

And the reality was that I had a chance!

My mind was very quiet. As the laps passed by, the only thing I could hear were my own thoughts and breathing.

Those and Marianne.

A Puncher's Chance

I had just finished my fifth lap. There were three more to go, and the leaders were 40 meters ahead of me. The way I felt physically was absolutely horrible. I've never felt so close to death, and that isn't an exaggeration.

My lungs were on fire. My legs were like Jell-O. My arms were the same. And I wanted to step off the track. Yet I will never forget seeing my father as he kept right on cheering for me, still standing by himself just a step away from the eighth lane at the top of the far stretch.

I looked right at him as if to say, "I have nothing left, Pops. I just can't do it." – one of the only times I made direct eye contact with him that whole run. So I had no choice but to see the intense excitement there. As if he knew something I didn't.

In a very matter-of-fact voice, he called out, "Michael, the leaders are dying. You have a chance here, Michael. You've got a chance!"

SEVEN

I had a chance.
"Now is the time to take it!"
Now is the time to take it.

I started thinking of the Steve Winwood song "While You See a Chance" and about all the times I'd listened to it before big races. As I headed down the backstretch, chasing the lead pack, I could hear the song playing in my head like a broken record.

"While you see a chance, take it."

The vision was coming alive before my very eyes. It was my story, and I was going to seize the moment. Even if it killed me.

Every big race has a crucial point where a runner either puts it all on the table or packs it up for the next year. This was the crucial point in my race, and my father knew it. Better yet, now I knew it too!

With that, I dropped my arms and cashed in everything I'd ever been saving. Passing Pop, I put my head down and went hunting for the lead pack.

Hit Light

As I approached the leaders with 1,000 meters left in the race, I didn't break stride. Marianne was yelling as I ran by, getting ready to take the lead. "Just drop your arms and hit light!"

It was my father's favorite thing to say at the critical part of a race.

"Hit light!" She called out again.

I could feel electricity in her voice and a definite new excitement in my other sisters' calls of encouragement as I ran by them – and then proceeded to pass the lead pack. I was in an all-out sprint when I went by them.

Not that they cared. They had their own strategies.

Most of the favorites in the race had a better kick than me, and they usually utilized it within the last 400 meters when they hit the bell lap. Kicking from 1,000 meters two and a half laps from the finish line was a long shot. Yet there I went anyway, taking a first-place position – no matter how temporarily – within a 200-meter stretch.

I was making my kick, and I was making it early. Very early. Yet it was now or never. I was a dark horse making a desperate move. And I did not mind that fact one bit. It didn't matter.

This was my only chance to steal the race.

Tomorrow, it's all about mind over matter.
If you don't mind, it doesn't matter.
– **Pop the night before the race**

Taking the lead, it was the worst and best I've ever felt in a race. I remember coming through the seventh lap with one left to go, that "last call" bell ringing in my ears. It was just like I'd pictured in my visions so many times.

Coming around the turn of the last lap, I could see Pop out of the corner of my eye. My vision was blurry, but I could see that he was bouncing up and down, almost as if he was a fighter dancing in place while he looked for the opportunity to land the perfect blow.

When I passed him, I knew I had to hold on for the longest 300 meters of my life. No matter how my legs felt. No matter how my lungs felt. No matter, because I had to put my head down and go hard into the headwind of that lonely backstretch.

My father just kept saying in a calm voice, "Hit light, Michael. Just hit light, son."

Meanwhile, five of my sisters had spread out a bit and were now standing along the backstretch. It was almost as if they were pulling me along the loneliest strip of land I'd ever run. I was running a dream race, but the reality of the field catching me was chasing me down with every step I took.

I could hear the runners behind me along with the reaction of the grandstands as I propelled my way to the finish line. It was pure electricity in the stadium. The energy was palpable, with my sisters fueling that power source.

Denise, Linda, Angela, Theresa and Marianne were screaming their heads off as my tired legs ate up the backstretch.

With 200 meters to go, I ran past them for the last time. And, knowing I had nothing left, they gave me everything they had.

The Vision Quest

They were all screaming so loudly for me. But once again, Marianne's voice stood out the most.

"This is it! This is it!" She shouted. "They're catching you, Michael! You have to kick now!"

SEVEN

Each word stood out as if the race depended on it. And it did.

"Get on your toes and go! Go now! Now, Michael! Now!"

I had never heard her yell so loud in all my life. It was like a jockey whipping her horse on the final stretch of the Kentucky Derby, except that Marianne was doing it through her words and not a stick.

She had pure fire in her voice. I don't know where it came from, but she scared me enough that I began to run with every ounce of life I had left in me. Reaching deep into the bank – all the way back to that spring when I was in third grade – I just put my head down and focused on the finish line with everything I had left.

It wasn't a lot.

I could faintly hear my father from across the track yelling, "Hit light and float!"

As I approached the finish line, I looked back to find that, somehow, someway, I'd held off the pack. The vision of me crossing the line looking up to Heaven in gratitude was coming true. I had seen it for the five weeks leading up to the race. Seen it so clearly that I'd drawn it repeatedly in my notebooks at school.

It was the vision quest my father had been reminding me of on a nightly basis.

And so I crossed that finish line in a wave of emotion, my arms extended upward and outward.

Going Out on Top

The dream was over, though I was still in a haze as I just kept jogging around to the 200-meter mark. I wanted to share the joy with my family immediately. In my mind, they had willed me to the finish line.

By then, my father had joined my sisters. I could see that much at least. I was sweating, my heart felt like it might honestly explode, my legs seemed close to death, and my lungs were almost literally on fire by my best guess.

None of that mattered. I wanted to see my sisters. Especially Marianne.

They had tears in their eyes when I ran up to them, and we all hugged and shared the moment. Marianne touched the pin she had given me only 15 minutes prior.

"We might have to retire this medal after that race. It's going out

on top!" she declared.
Little did she know that she was 100% correct. One year and a day later, Patti received it when she had her twin daughters, Alessandra and Olivia. And from then on, the medal was reserved for such bigger and better moments, because all my sisters had it with them when they gave birth.

One thing is for sure: It ended its running career on a high note. Its final race was a definite win, and one made possible by the Lord alone.

It took me six weeks to recover from that venture, but it was well worth the effort.

A Little Faith

Marianne has made a trend of being a bright light in the world. She displayed that gift while encouraging me to run in the first place. She did it again during that race of a lifetime. And, sure enough she was shining bright that Christmas morning in the hospital.

Really, that day, she couldn't have been shining brighter.

As she stood over Pop, I remembered every moment I'd ever seen her shine. It was as if our heavenly Father had trained her for that very moment. He instilled so much faith into her that she was easily – naturally – able to give it right back at someone's lowest.

As Pop said during his recovery, "That Marianne gave me faith, and you know what the Bible says about faith. With it you can move mountains."

After Linda's life was saved by Marianne one fateful fall day, she stated, "Marianne is pure light," and I think she was right. This sister of ours gave Pop the ability to see strongly enough to get back into the race.

I think he summed it up best during one of our walks and talks during his comeback. "That Marianne just has a way of painting things. She's like a Michelangelo of visions."

She's a constant reminder that, if you ever need a little faith, all you need to do is remember to stay in the light and keep your sight on the vision our Father has for you.

Like Pop used to call out at the most crucial points of the race, "Just hit light and float."

The rest will come to you.

CHAPTER 9
Theresa: The Blooming Flower

Love

The sun had just risen when Marianne gave me a light shove on the shoulder and told me it was time to get up for work.

Rubbing my eyes, I groggily worked my way out of bed, trying to make my 12-year-old, non-morning-person brain function.

The first thing I noticed when I got to my feet was that my other roommate wasn't actually in the room. "Where's Theresa?"

"She woke up early to get her run in," Marianne answered.

I moved the shades back to let the light brighten the room and help me wake up a little more. The sun was just coming up on what was sure to be a very hot summer day, so Theresa was getting her workout in before it could prove as much, before the customers started rolling in for fresh produce, and before the commotion of another long work day began in our driveway.

As I was standing at the window, stretching my arms in the air, I saw a small figure in the distance getting closer with every step. Far off in the back field, it was Theresa finishing her run.

I quickly put on shorts, shirt and shoes, and went to the field to run striders with her. The field behind our house, where we did most of our training, was owned by our neighbor, Scott. He was just a couple years older than Joey, and Pop was like a father figure to him. So we could use the field anytime we liked. In fact, Scott said he enjoyed us running around his field. It was 17-acres of plush grass surrounded by pine trees, blue spruce and wooden fences.

When we were kids, we did laps around it all the time. The small ones we measured at 400 meters were known as "Small Scott Laps," and four of those made a mile. The "Large Scott Lap," meanwhile, was 1,000 meters – the equivalent of two and a half laps around a real track.

Growing up, we did most of our training and interval workouts in that field because Pop said it was better for our legs, easier on the knees and would make us stronger. Plus, we could run barefoot, which we sometimes liked to do. We stayed off the roads as much as possible because roads can put a lot of wear and tear on the body's joints.

Theresa and I called it "The Field of Dreams" after one of my favorite baseball movies. As our father would often say when he was training us there, "If there's a place to run in Heaven, I bet it looks a lot like this."

Theresa and I truly felt it was a slice of running paradise. And nobody did more laps around our bit of heaven than she did. She was the archangel in that heavenly track.

A Coach's Dream

Theresa always ended her runs with 200-meter striders to shake out her legs. We used to refer to them as our "jog, stride, sprints," and Theresa never skipped them. By the time I got out to the field, she was already clipping off her fourth.

"Hey, Mikey, do you want to run the last four with me?" She asked with excitement in her voice, barely breathing hard as I approached her, a testament to the kind of shape she was in.

I could smell the freshly cut grass as the sun slowly rose.

"I'll watch you run one, and then I'll jump in the last three," I replied. "I need to save some energy. Mommy said it's going to be really busy today." And closing time at 6:00 was still a very long way away.

"Good," was her response. "The day goes by faster when it's

busy."

With that, she took off running. As she did, I couldn't help but think that Pop was right about her. He'd told me one time, "Theresa is a coach's dream and a competitor's nightmare."

That really did sum her up when it came to running. Personally, I was just happy I was a boy and would never have to face her on the track. People who had to race her should be pitied.

She was born to run and hated to lose.

Full Potential

One of my earliest memories of Theresa was watching her run Scott Laps with Pop.

She would flat-out fly when she got moving, and she seriously loved to run. Once she hit about eight or nine years old, there was no stopping her. She just enjoyed the very act of running, letting her body move like it wanted to.

Like so many sports, running is an activity where spectators not only watch what athletes can do in the heat of the moment, but also what kind of spirit they have deep inside when the race is on the line.

That is why sports in general are so big in this country and the entire world. They can inspire and motivate people like no one else can, and can show us the full potential of the human body in all its glory.

In Theresa's case, she trained like a contender going for the title, improving constantly with everything she did throughout the day. Yet she wasn't obsessed with running, at least not in a way that interfered with the rest of her life. She worked both the produce business and Christmas tree business, and she worked tirelessly. She never slacked.

Whenever I finished up a job, I'd inevitably want to take a break. But not Theresa. She just kept on moving. She didn't like to stop and rest, and she rarely complained.

Springs for Legs and Wings on Her Shoes

Theresa and I have gone through the highs and lows of life side by side just like so many of the many meters we've run. They were our trials through the miles.

I've seen her in times of absolute triumph, and I've seen her in complete despair. But throughout all of it, she taught me about the courageous spirit we human beings are capable of achieving, where we refuse to quit and accept nothing but the best.

Growing up, I don't remember many runs I did where Theresa wasn't right beside me or a few steps ahead. We would talk and share our dreams as we blazed around the track or through the fields behind our house. So I know straight from the racehorse's mouth that she was very clear in what she wanted out of running.

She wanted to win, capture state titles, and then run in college. Just like Denise.

"When I get my chance, I'm going to try to break every record in the state," she once told me during a cooldown after one of my father's famous workouts at the track.

We were just kids at the time, still years away from the spotlight. But she had it in her heart that when the day did arrive for her to set foot on the big stage, she would take her chance and run with it. Always dreaming. Always pushing the pace. Never going easy in runs if she didn't have to. That was my sister Theresa. Yet always so gracious in her execution.

"Come on, Michael!" she would shout. "Try to just keep up with me. Run behind me, and let me do the work."

She genuinely wouldn't mind.

"I'll block the wind for you on the backstretch; just tuck in behind me! Someday, you'll be a champion too. I just know it!"

Theresa often said things like that to me, offering encouragements that got me through many a run.

Born to Run

Out of everyone, Theresa looked up to Denise the most in the family. She was her big sister and her godmother, and they had a strong emotional bond.

Their bodies were also built the same, with small torsos, long legs and great turnover. Plus, they both had a glide in their stride that made it appear like they were floating when they ran at top speed. The faster they ran, the more relaxed they looked.

They were both built for running, but no one loved racing more than Theresa. Like all great athletes, she shone brightest when it counted most.

For her big races, Theresa would write "Isaiah 40" on the side of one shoe. It's her favorite Bible verse, with verses 28-41 reading like this:

> Do you not know?
> Have you not heard?
> The Lord is the everlasting God,
> the Creator of the ends of the earth.
> He will not grow tired or weary,
> and his understanding no one can fathom.
> He gives strength to the weary
> and increases the power of the weak.
> Even youths grow tired and weary,
> and young men stumble and fall;
> but those who hope in the Lord
> will renew their strength.
> They will soar on wings like eagles;
> they will run and not grow weary,
> they will walk and not be faint.

A Great One Comes Along Every 10 Years

Theresa ran with a purpose. She'd learned to do so from Denise. She knew the price it took to be the best, and she was willing to pay it.

Some athletes have the "it" factor. We've seen it in so many greats throughout the years. It's hard to miss in those cases, and Theresa was one of those cases! When she was a little girl, Pop had to hold her back because he was afraid she'd hurt herself if she ran the way she liked to run for as long as she liked to run. But by the time she hit fifth grade, she was ready to fly.

Theresa was literally off and running.

Even at the young age of 11, she was training with the intensity of an NCAA athlete. She saw Denise do it, and she decided to do it even better.

When Denise trained, she trained with a certain precision. Each day had a purpose and a goal that was meant to lead in to a bigger goal – usually a championship race. This meant that, sometimes, she paced herself on purpose.

The difference with Theresa was twofold. One, she rarely took it easy in her training unless expressly told to. And two, she started at a younger age.

The hidden field behind our house was where she discovered her true gift in running. It was away from the spotlight that Theresa discovered her greatness. As Pop would tell me when we watched title-fight boxing matches, "Champions don't become champions in the ring. They're just recognized there."

Hitting the Ground

Even with 11 kids and a full-time job that consisted of not one but two businesses, my father would still lace up his running shoes for a quick run when he got home. He didn't have time for races and marathons, of course, but he loved the act of running and so he did it on his own. Until Theresa came along.

As a child, she would wait for him to get home every day, her running gear already on and her feet ready to fly. Then she'd run stride for stride with him as they looped our neighbor's 17-acre field.

Out of all my sisters, Theresa was the quietest. Like Kate, she stayed out of any commotion in the house. Yet while she was meek most of the time, she was loud as thunder when she raced.

She just didn't like to run slow. She preferred to push the pace, whether it was in a race or when she was training. Her mentality with running was just like Pop's. If you're going to race fast, you have to train fast. It was that simple.

Pop used to talk about seeing Secretariat's 1973 Triple-Crown win and witnessing greatness. Well, people said the same about Theresa. She had two legs instead of four, but she was flat-out amazing nonetheless. If you saw her run one time, you'd never forget it.

When she raced, it didn't even look like she was hitting the ground, and she would speed up as she went. Because Theresa didn't run. She floated, with wings on her shoes.

In the running world, Theresa was what you could call a "once in a decade" type of runner. That term is usually used in boxing to explain how a great one comes along every 10 years, with it being up to the spectators to recognize that person. Yet it applies just as well on the track as in the ring.

People would compare Denise and Theresa like boxing fans

compared Marciano and Ali. The older sister may have had a steadier career than her younger sibling's roller coaster one. But in her prime, Theresa was quite simply untouchable.

As a news reporter once eloquently stated after a race, "Theresa Marini is pure beauty in motion."

The Running Archive

Because we all had competed or were competing in the same sport, it was easy and natural to swap stories and advice on the subject. The training, the races and the proper diets – all the way down to what got us psyched up before a race. Running was just a popular topic.

At my family's collective running peak, we had one competing in college, two in high school, and three in grade school. With that many races and seasons, we were naturally never short on running stories.

Since Theresa and I were numbers nine and 10 in line, we got to hear so many stories growing up about our older siblings' favorite running moments. Theresa was a true pupil of the sport, and she knew every story inside and out. Usually, she was shy and reserved when she spoke. But not when it came to running.

When it came to running, she just wasn't short on words.

When Theresa talked about running and the goals she wanted to reach, she was very matter of fact. She wanted to be downright unstoppable, and she couldn't wait until she got her own chance on the big stage. As early as fourth grade, Theresa was talking about being a state champion.

Her goals were simple: She wanted to break records and win big races.

Running Down a Dream

When Theresa was in sixth-grade, there was a high school freshman who was tearing up all the records. No one was even close to this girl in any of her races.

Since Danny and Jimmy were both running in high school at the time, Theresa and I went to a lot of their meets. And that meant we got to see this record-breaker win over and over again.

"No one's ever going to beat that girl," I said as she blew by us on her way to her first state title, winning by over 45 seconds.

"I will," Theresa stated very quietly.

It wasn't her usual running-related voice that time. She said it almost in a whisper, as if she didn't even want me to hear her.

But I did. And I laughed. "What are you going to do? Take a shortcut or something?"

That did it for Theresa though. She looked me straight in the eyes this time. "No. She slows down on the hills. I love hills; they're my favorite."

She had a point. Even in the sixth grade, she was strong on hills. Most of the time, runners will slow down when they run up a hill, but Theresa wasn't like most runners. She would speed up on those obstacles.

When she did, she looked like a deer in an open field, bounding along with such ease, lifting her knees and pumping her arms the whole way.

Theresa used hills to punish her competition. To break them. To gain ground.

It was a great skill and strategy to have.

The Great One That Can Run

As we watched runners slowly funnel into the finish that day, we stretched and did striders to get ready for our own scheduled runs along the very same course. A course where, three years later, Theresa would end up racing that record-breaking girl for the state title.

She already knew the date. "Saturday November 12."

Once again, it came out as a soft whisper, this time as we passed the one-mile mark.

They always run the state meet the second week in November, and Theresa had looked it up on a calendar already. She knew exactly how long she had to get ready to take on this girl who couldn't be beat.

After we passed the two-mile mark, she told me exactly how she'd run against the girl and where she would make her moves. The first attack would be on what everyone referred to as "The Stair Case", and she would go for the kill on "Bunker Hill."

That last one was about a half-mile out from the finish line, and many races had been won and lost on it. People with huge leads would sometimes die out on that brutally slanted stretch. It was known to take front runners and reduce them to losers in a quarter-mile. So Theresa understood, if she could just stay with her extreme competition until Bunker Hill, she could take the whole thing.

When she talked about it, she didn't have one doubt in her mind that she would beat this girl the newspapers had dubbed "The Great One That Can Run." One article even talked about her possibly being the first four-time cross country State champion, and she was crowned the greatest runner the state had ever seen – in her freshman year.

To many people, that notion wasn't going to change anytime soon.

The War Plan

As we were finishing our run, we ran past this so-called Great One who was even then talking to reporters. Yet Theresa didn't so much as look at her.

The same couldn't be said about the Great One.

I saw that girl regarding us as we went by, with Theresa way out in front of me. She'd shifted into a higher gear for the last stretch, and she'd done so with enough drive to catch her one-day competitor's attention.

Struggling to catch my breath after such a tough run, I still managed to send a joke Theresa's way. "It looks like 'The Great One' was watching you. Maybe she's scared."

There was no hesitation to her reply. "I would be if I was her."

As we walked away, she was saying how she couldn't wait to race that girl.

"Do you really think you can do it?" I asked. "I mean, coming in second to her wouldn't be that bad."

But Theresa wasn't concerned at all about that. To her, it was a non-possibility when she had "over a thousand days to train for it."

Call It

Theresa religiously did her push-ups, sit ups, and stretching every night. Like a few of my other sisters, she was like an ant when it came to her body strength. All her years of working the produce and Christmas businesses – those long days filled with lifting boxes of fruit and bushels of corn during the summer and hoisting trees and bundles of greens during the holidays – came through in every step she took when she ran.

Push-ups, sit-ups, stretching and arm weights were all part of her usual routine. While the rest of the family was sitting around, watching TV, Theresa would be in the corner of the living room doing her exercises.

Getting a seat and keeping it in my household was a big deal when we watched TV. If you left the room without saying, "Call it," your seat would be taken. No ifs, ands or buts about it. It was a rule, and everyone followed it to the letter.

But Theresa never bothered with those words because Theresa never claimed a seat in the first place. The days clipped by, and she simply stuck with her plan.

Pre-Greatness

Seventh grade quickly turned into eighth grade for her, during which time we were training together most days. Besides baseball practice, not much could keep me from running with Theresa.

In the process, I was seeing her progress every day. Her stride was increasing, she was running with more power, and it appeared she was forming springs in her legs. Before she was sharing class space with them, Theresa was running better than most of the kids in high school. And it appeared she had lots more in the tank.

The times she was running by the end of eighth grade were based off that basic training Pop instilled in us – in other words, not much traditional training at all. So once she started doing some serious preparation, she'd be able to run some pretty quick times.

As the table got set for Theresa to enter high school, I couldn't wait to see what was in store for her.

We'd heard so many classic stories about our older siblings by then. Now Theresa wanted to add to the repertoire of legendary tales told around the kitchen table.

Before You Know It

In horse racing, they say that some horses just have it in their blood: that nose for the finish line. And with boxing, there's that great one who comes along every 10 years.

When Theresa started high school, "the great one" was already there. This was a girl who'd already proved that she'd never see the back of another runner her entire career.

Or at least the first three years.

"The Great One" didn't know that the little girl she'd seen sprinting to the finish line in a training run three years prior was about to make her work for it.

Theresa had stuck to her plan and trained that whole time. She wasn't doing any crazy training, but she was honed nonetheless. Pop would keep our runs short and sweet – a lot of striders and focusing on form.

Before high school, we were conditioned to expect runs to be light and fun. When it came time to race, you turned it on, of course. But otherwise, it was very low-key for Theresa and me. Pop purposely held us back in our training when we were kids because he knew the hard running that was ahead of us, and he liked to "keep it fresh."

When an athlete competes in high school or college, much more is asked of them. They need to put in more time and harder training, with more focus on all the little things that manage to make the biggest difference on race days. Things like getting the right amount of sleep, eating right, getting plenty of fluids, doing the proper stretching, and strengthening to have your body at its peak when you feel like you're in the valley halfway through a race.

Our father ingrained this in us from an early age and he would tell us our best running was still to come. That's how he prepared us for high school and college.

"Keep it fresh, keep it light and keep it fun," he would stress to us when we were young. "The big races are far off now; but believe me, they'll be here before you know it. We're just putting hay in the barn for later years when you'll need it most."

Then he'd add, "Remember, it's better to be stocked up come winter time than to not be stocked up."

He was the Yogi Berra and Knute Rockne of the running world, and Theresa was one of his greatest pupils.

Our Trials Through the Miles

Pop seemed to have a term for each one of our running styles, and to him, Theresa was a "heart runner." In that regard, she was definitely cut from the same mold as Denise. They had different strides and forms when running, but they still managed to race the exact same way.

To win.

Here's an interesting insight about running. It's a sport that doesn't allow you to hide any weaknesses. When you're on the track, people can see every step you take, the pain in your face and the fear in your eyes. There is no way of covering such things up.

Running is one of the few sports where it's not just a person's physical ability on display; it's also their spirit.

That meant it was doubly beautiful to watch Theresa run. She had a fighting spirit that refused to quit, and it shone particularly bright in high school. Like she'd told me she would back when we were children, Theresa made sure to seize her time when it arrived.

She wasn't just any average or stereotypical runner when she entered high school. She was 4'11 and 89 lbs. But she only knew one gear, and that was fifth.

Theresa was a genuine thrill to watch run. People had thought Denise was a wonder, and she was. But Theresa was a whole other beast altogether. She took the running world by storm.

While no one in the state knew how good she really was when she first started running, she changed that. Fast. By the middle of her freshman year, she was already rewriting the record books – definitely something to talk about.

Then again, she hadn't yet taken on the best runner in Delaware and one of the best in the country, someone who hadn't been beaten for three consecutive years. "The Great One" had already won the states three times by then. So while everyone could see how impressive Theresa was, most people automatically assumed she wasn't on par against her older, more experienced competition.

I remember how nervous Theresa was the night before she ran against the defending state champ that first time. In fact, she was quiet the whole week before it. More quiet than usual, that is.

It was her first true test.

Tougher Than the Rest

The drizzle hit Mom's windshield as Bruce Springsteen's *Tunnel of Love* tape played softly through the car speakers. My mom liked

SEVEN

that album so much, she kept it in the tape deck of her black 1984 Honda Accord for over two years. It's all she would listen to when she drove.

"Tougher Than the Rest" is the second song on the album, and it was playing that day as we pulled into the park where the showdown would take place.

I remember how jumpy I felt for this particular race. For some reason, I usually got more nervous before my sisters' races then I did for my own. And this one was the most nervous I ever got. My heart was full-out pounding as we approached the Carpenter State Park sign. This would be Theresa's real unveiling, and I knew it.

All those days she, Marianne and I ran through the little town of Arden near our house were now meant to pay off. Whenever we had training runs there, my sisters would say it was like running through an *Alice in Wonderland* scene. Every house was different, and people would wave as "the Marini kids" ran by.

Could this be another dream-world setting?

We'd soon find out.

A Shot at the Title

When we got to the race, I took my place at the two-mile point just as planned. It was a 5K (3.1-mile), so being at the two-mile mark was perfect. I could see the beginning that way, then hang out for 12 minutes until they ran by me. At that point, I could move to another spot to watch the rest of the race and still catch the finish.

Standing there as everyone lined up, I remember thinking how small Theresa looked compared to the defending champion. And once the gun went off, I knew it was going to be a battle.

As they headed into the woods, there was Theresa and the best runner in the state running stride for stride. Within no time at all, they had 40 meters on the pack.

The one-on-one bout had started right away.

Like two fighters trying to knock each other out in the very first round, they were both bringing their best. As I watched them fade into the woods, I knew Theresa was in a pure moment of truth.

A Star Is Born

For the next 12 minutes, I stood at that two-mile mark, holding onto my baseball glove and ball. While I threw the ball in the air and caught it over and over again, I had a million thoughts racing through my mind.

Theresa was running somewhere in those woods – her heart pounding, her legs burning, her lungs screaming. And the person side by side with her hadn't been beaten in three years.

I continued to throw the ball until I heard the people in the woods starting to cheer. It hadn't seemed like very long when I heard the screaming.

"Here she comes! Here she comes!"

It was the voice of a coach from another team who was just there to see the big showdown. This guy was the Rain Man of running in our state. He could rattle off times and useless stats about most runners who had ever run in Delaware. Usually, he didn't speak unless spoken to. But now he was yelling at the top of his lungs.

"She's got 17 seconds on her! *She's got 17 seconds!*"

I could hear him before I could see the frontrunners, and my heart dropped to my feet. This Great One didn't just want to beat my sister, it seemed. She wanted to crush her.

Or maybe Theresa just couldn't keep up. Maybe she took a wrong turn.

Shocking

She hadn't though. Not even close.

Theresa wasn't 17 seconds behind the champion. She was 17 seconds ahead of her.

There she was, flying along with such beauty and grace that I found myself laughing as she ran by me.

"Are you kidding me?" I yelled at her.

She didn't look my way, too busy trying to set a course record. Which I certainly wasn't going to stand in the way of.

The "Rain Man of Running" was utterly shocked. "She isn't just going to beat her; she's going to set a course record! Yeah, a course record. I can't believe it!"

From there, he started to mumble, making it difficult to know whether he was talking to me or to himself. "I can't believe it. No one's even come close to beating that girl in three years. But she's crushing her. I can't believe it!"

It truly was a sight to be seen. One of the best runners the state had ever seen looked like a jogger compared to Theresa, who was gliding along with seemingly no effort. I remember watching everyone stare at Theresa in absolute amazement while her legs ate up the track. No one knew what to think. It was like watching a shooting star fly past me straight on to the finish line.

But that shooting star didn't stop to bask in the awe radiating around her. After she finished, she turned right around to jog back to the final stretch. She wanted to cheer for Marianne, who was in a battle of her own for third place.

That's just how Theresa shone, even at her brightest moments.

Onward, Upward and Beyond

That October day was a major moment for Theresa, but it wasn't her only one. She went on to set more records and capture the state title too, just like she said she would back in sixth grade. Most weekends, she was running in big meets in Pennsylvania, New York or Maryland, and her and Marianne's pictures were in the newspapers on a weekly basis.

Theresa had a lot of fans, one of them being an Italian-American reporter who wrote for the local paper. He followed her entire high school and college career. His articles had a way of putting Theresa's greatness into the sort of black and white you could read with your Sunday coffee.

After she ran a record time at Brandywine Creek State Park, one of the hilliest courses on the East Coast, the reporter wrote, "She looked like she was running downhill with the wind at her back from the gun until she crossed the finish line."

One of the many great races of her running career was when she won the cross country state championship her sophomore year. A local reporter had gone on record predicting an M-O-M – Marini, Opperman, Marini – finish, since Theresa had come in third for the county championship the week before. Yet she came back to redeem herself, proving she was still at the top of her game.

She stayed that way the whole year too, running well, getting good grades and focusing on her future goals. But during her junior year, things started to change, seemingly for the worse.

She had overall dominated for two years straight. But now she was about to see the other side of her running career.

Growing up, she hated Pop's prescribed recovery running days when she couldn't run fast. She adhered to them, but she hated them. Unfortunately, I suppose that larger love of speed became her undoing, with injuries piling up one by one until she had to stop running altogether after college.

Even so, Theresa had the longest competitive running career in the family – about 15 years. She ran through the ups and downs, refusing to quit until there was no other choice in the matter. Running was her passion. Her true love.

And throughout it, she's showed me the courage in her spirit. The latter part of her track experience wouldn't be about setting records and being a sure-shot to take first place. It would be about determination, which was just as worthwhile to behold.

Growing Pains

As Theresa's body kept growing in high school, she continued to train hard. Yet running the way she was at the rate her body was developing made for a bad formula, leaving her constantly trying to figure out "what was wrong."

This happens with some female runners. As their hips begin to widen, it changes the angle the hip sits above the knee, known as the "Q angle." This can then lead to back, knee and ankle problems, making once-easy runs something far from it.

In Theresa's case, it was so hard to see her trying 10 times harder yet achieving so few obvious rewards from those intense efforts. For a while there, I couldn't help but feel so frustrated every time I watched. I knew the deer in her wanted to run, but it was injured. Her spirit wanted to fly, but her body wouldn't let her. In many ways, this experience helped to form her into the incredible coach she is today.

Yet way back then, she continued to battle anyway. That was just who she was.

Her True Spirit

It was the state championship at Brandywine Creek State Park her senior year. After everything was run and done, Theresa went off to find an isolated bench, where she sat silently with her eyes closed.

I had followed her into the woods to make sure she was safe. But

SEVEN

as I stood back and watched her, I saw her shine without even knowing it as she began to cry. She'd just finished her final high school cross country race. But unlike two years earlier, she hadn't won.

She had planned for it so intensely, hoping to make it her big comeback, only to find that it wouldn't – couldn't – pan out the way she wanted it to.

Watching her that day, I felt guilty for being so sad that she'd had a bad race. I thought it made me a sore loser how upset I was. Looking back though, I now know my feelings went much deeper than a mere title.

It never had anything to do with the running. Theresa's spirit – her soul – was hurting, and I felt it. My sister was sad, and I was sad with her. Watching her heart break was breaking my own.

It was perhaps also the first time I saw her true spirit on full display. Because there she was, away from everyone else. No spotlight. No photographers. No reporters asking her questions. She wasn't demanding that people look her way or feel pity for her while she wept. She just wept in the same way she used to "just win."

Theresa took defeat the same way she took victory. Graciously.

Love on Your Side

Anyone who watches *The Wizard of Oz* learns that the lion didn't need some mighty being to give him courage. He had it inside him the whole time; he just needed to discover it. Someone to point it out.

Don't we all?

So very often, that's Theresa. She brings her quiet type of ability wherever she goes, including at the hospital while she sat with Pop that Christmas morning.

She reminded him that he was just like the lion in Oz. That all the gifts he needed were already right there in his heart.

I firmly believe that she's the one who got through to him the most that Christmas morning. He needed her most that day, and she didn't fail him, shining brighter than I could have ever imagined.

Our Theresa was at her best in such a big race, just like Pop had trained her. She brought the biggest gift to him that day: the gift of love. And with that seemingly simple gift in its proper place, you will not lose.

Pop certainly didn't.

Theresa is a consistently shining reminder that, when we get knocked down, there's still something so very worthwhile to be had.

Before my sisters left the hospital room that Christmas morning, Pop took a long sip of water and cleared his throat.

Then he said, "Every day, I really try to do my best for the good Lord. I get up early and work hard. Though sometimes I stumble if I don't follow God's lead."

He paused for a brief moment, though not in contemplation about the failures he'd just mentioned. His focus was already set on bigger and better things, as his next words revealed.

"But when I listen, I can see it all and it's so simple. He loves us, and the times I know it most are the times I'm at my best."

I have no doubt that Theresa inspired that sentiment in him. She gave him love; and with love on your side, nothing is impossible.

CHAPTER 10
Angela: The Little Angel

Joy

As the emcee handed the microphone over to my father, the crowd of 250 became completely silent.

"Today is my graduation day!" He said with a big smile on his face.

It was Angela's wedding day, and Pop had just married off his seventh daughter. In commemoration of such a momentous event, he gave the greatest speech of his life, quoting songs, reciting a poem and sounding like he was offering a motivational address instead of a mere toast.

"Life and marriage are about ordinary people doing extraordinary things," he declared. "With the Lord in your corner, nothing is impossible. He makes anything possible. It's simple when you get right down to it."

Every eye was on him.

"Look at Noah, for example," he continued. "He was a simple guy who built an ark. Then you jump ahead thousands of years to the guys who built the *Titanic*. They were all big-time engineers with fancy degrees who thought they could do anything."

He paused perfectly. "Well, we know how those two stories

end."

The crowd erupted in laughter.

After the laughter faded, Pop put his head down for a moment. And then he began to sing.

It was off-key. But that didn't much matter in the moment.

> *I hear babies cry.*
> *I watch them grow.*
> *They'll learn much more than I'll ever know.*
> *And I think to myself what a wonderful world.*
> *Yes, I think to myself… what a wonderful world!*

With those lines from Louis' Armstrong's "What a Wonderful World" concluded, he thanked everyone for coming, gave the microphone back to the emcee and slowly walked back to his chair.

The entire room stood up to give him a standing ovation.

Don Corleone might have had one "day of my daughter's wedding." But my father had seven.

The Big Announcement

Angela can't be called a surprise baby. She was simply a miracle baby.

The night we found out we were getting yet another member to the family, Marianne, Theresa and I were sitting on the couch watching TV. It had been a long day selling Christmas trees, and we were all grateful to be resting our legs and backs and brains.

I was just six years old with a full head of curly black hair, but I did know a few things back then. I knew I loved *The Incredible Hulk* and the Philadelphia Phillies. And I knew I absolutely loved being the youngest in the family.

It was my position in the family. My identity, if you will.

Plus, being the youngest had its perks at such a young age. My sisters' friends would tell me how cute I was. People pinched my cheeks. I got lots of hugs and little presents here and there. And I didn't think it was ever going to change.

My position as the youngest was securely fastened in my mind. Everyone else's too.

Mom was well into her 40s by then, after all, with a full brood of 10 children. It would therefore take a near-impossible roll of the dice for me to lose my loved and lauded position.

The Vegas oddsmakers would have called it a long shot for my mom to get pregnant yet again at the age of 45. But odds never seemed to matter with her. Like she had done her whole life, she just went and beat 'em.

What a Wonderful World

My first clue that things were going to be changing soon enough was the commotion coming from the kitchen.

Now, commotion was very normal in our house. But this was more of an uncontrolled commotion. A mystery that had to be solved! So I grabbed my Incredible Hulk action figure and headed toward the kitchen.

It was completely out of control in there!

My parents weren't in the room, but everyone else was swarming around Patti. So whatever the information was, she had it. Which made her a very big deal.

Information in my house was like gold. When you had "the dirt," as my family calls it, you had control of the entire room. You were center stage.

Generally speaking, Patti was one of the best when it came to filling us in on any dirt. So, generally speaking, Patti had complete control of the room.

She definitely did right then.

"What happened?" I wanted to know "the dirt" too! "Why is everyone yelling?"

But my questions went ignored, and I couldn't make much out on my own except how Patti had "overheard Mommy and Daddy talking, and they are going to announce something. Something REALLY BIG!"

As such, rumors were flying around the room, ranging from whether we were moving to maybe our German Shepherd, Dawn, was being put to sleep. Even so, we did settle down enough to take seats around the kitchen table by the time our parents' bedroom door opened.

The footsteps we heard as Pop walked down the hallway into the kitchen were so familiar. Yet, clearly, he was bringing with him something unfamiliar – good or bad – this time around.

Right behind him was my mother. And the second I saw her

face, I could tell she had some major "dirt."

A Game Changer

One of the few negatives of being the youngest was that I was usually told to leave the room if something serious was being discussed. And I did not want to miss this dirt! So to be on the safe side, I hid in the dining room next to the kitchen. There, trying not to make any noise from my secret spot behind a chair, I could overhear everything without anyone knowing.

But apparently I played it a little too safe, because all I heard was mumbling. And then an absolute eruption!

I had missed it!

Racing into the kitchen, I was met with complete pandemonium.

"What happened?" I yelled. "What did she say?"

No one could hear me though. Again.

It was the most excitement I'd ever seen in that kitchen, which said a lot coming from an excitable Italian family. I tried getting to Mom, but she was completely surrounded by my brothers and sisters, who were acting completely out of control.

Finally, I couldn't stand it anymore and proceeded to yell at the top of my lungs, "What did she say!"

Without further ado, the room got quiet. Very, very quiet until Patti grabbed me and put me up on the table.

Nothing could have prepared my fragile six-year old eggshell mind for the news.

The End of My Reign

"Michael, you're going to be an older brother!"

The room lost control all over again, utterly overwhelming me in the process. I was being hugged and kissed, and everyone was talking and shouting and laughing and crying. But I was completely confused.

How will there be two youngest children?

With all the commotion, I couldn't think. It just did not sink into my brain in those first few seconds. I needed some time to process this.

I didn't want to be hugged. I wanted to think. My personal space was being invaded, and I was starting to lose it.

Then it hit me.

"You mean I won't be the youngest anymore?" It was something between a bewildered question and an outraged demand.

No one heard me. They were too busy celebrating.

It was a devastating night for me, bringing with it a slew of questions not easily explained to a six-year-old. How could this have happened? How could I have been dethroned from my solidly cushy position?

It took weeks for it to sink in as, all the while, my reign as The Youngest slowly ended. Mom's belly reminded me of my impending doom a bit more every day. For the next seven months of my life, I would be in the "lame duck" position of youngest child in the Marini family.

And I couldn't do anything about it.

The "7-11" Baby

I love when my mother tells the story about giving birth to my little sister – how everyone kept peeking their head in the room just to get a glimpse of the "woman who was having her 11th child." The same doctor who delivered her previous 10 even came out of retirement for the occasion.

There was so much excitement that day, with everyone waiting for the call as we worked. It was mid-summer, and our family produce market was in full swing. Open seven days a week, nine hours a day, it was keeping all of us older siblings – myself included – physically busy while everyone awaited The Call.

All the bets were already in on whether it was a boy or a girl. Would we have a queen or a king taking over my cushy throne?

Seven's Heaven

In many religions and cultures, certain numbers are considered lucky, and seven is certainly one of them. Some even believe it's a holy number, since it took God seven days to create the world, in which he ultimately sliced out seven continents and divided them by seven seas.

Others will say there are seven spirits of God and seven archangels. And God didn't work five days and then rest. He worked six days and rested on the seventh. His day.

Seven happened to be a big number in my family too, even well before the seventh day of the seventh month when my seventh sister came home from the hospital. Looking at this little one-day-old bundle, my family knew we'd been sent an angel from above.

Even I had to recognize that. And I was just seven years old.

The Seven Sisters

My grandfather used to say that God was the best author in the world. In his broken English, he would state, "God, he-ah always put-ta in a happy ending."

Well, taking in the sight of my little sister on the day she came home from the hospital, I couldn't help but see how God had done amazing authorial work with this particular part of the text. He was doing a heck of a job with my family's story, and I could not wait to see what He was going to write next.

Looking over his full brood that week, Pop felt like a farmer gazing out onto a beautiful, bountiful field he knew would harvest wonderful fruits and vegetables. "It looks like we have a heck of a crop this year!" he declared.

And so we did. The table was finally set, and the family was complete for a while. The last piece of the foundation had been put in place.

Angela, the seventh girl and eleventh kid, had made her official appearance to round out the full family into our very own baker's dozen.

Angel Angela

She's the little angel
So innocent and sweet
She's the little angel
Now the family is complete
  – One of my poems at age 7

Angela has kind of been a celebrity in the family ever since the first day she came. She brings a whole new level of energy to the family when she's present. Really, what she brings is joy.

Joy is one of God's greatest gifts to us. He loves to fill our hearts with it down here on earth if we only choose to receive it, and it awaits us in even greater portions when we enter the gates of Heaven as well.

It's important to recognize, however, that joy and happiness aren't the same thing, no matter how people tend to think of them as synonymous.

Angela certainly wasn't happy about our father's near-death situation when she came sweeping into his hospital room right behind her fellow shining stars. But there's no denying the joy she brought with her.

That Christmas morning, she had an energy that lifted my father, my sisters and the entire staff.

Any Other Way

She is "the little Angel"
My little sister is very small
Baby angels are not very tall
She has little feet
She sits in my old car seat
She sleeps with a nightlight
It keeps me up at night

Whenever we eat, she makes a mess
Last week, she threw up on my Mommy's Easter dress
She cries a lot, but that is okay
She is the little Angel, and I wouldn't want it any other way
– One of my poems in second-grade

Born Leader

Once Angela decided to talk, we all found out she had a lot to say. She let you know just what she thought, so if she didn't like what was going on, the whole family was going to know about it.

Believe you me.

My parents had perhaps been spoiled a little bit by Marianne and Theresa's quiet natures. But for the first few years after she learned to speak, Angela showed no indication of heading in that direction.

She was doing things her way or no way. This new youngest child was using her status beautifully, and I couldn't help but be impressed.

It wasn't until she entered kindergarten that she seemed to quiet down quite a bit. It seemed as if, after saying what she had to say, Angela just slowly stepped out of the spotlight of her own choosing. Like me, she took on the position of watching, listening and learning instead.

It was a habit that would teach her about love, life, family and relationships, and help her cultivate compassion, which today is one of her best qualities. It may be a lot easier to get bodies moving when you speak more, but it's much easier to get souls moving when you listen more.

And so my baby sister developed an enormous sense of empathy for people, as well as the ability to assess, address and handle any situation that came her way. She became truly stellar at all three.

No matter that she wasn't stating her opinions nearly as much as she once did, Angela still wasn't anyone's idea of a follower. No matter that she was the youngest of 11 either.

That girl is a leader through and through.

Groundhog Day

Most weekday mornings of my grade-school career started the same – with me sleeping in perhaps a little too late. And it didn't get any better in junior high. By then, I was solidly set in my patterns and was an absolute bear to wake up.

My mother would have to practically yank me by my ankles to get me out of bed.

Despite her best efforts to make a positive difference in this area, it wasn't Mom who kept me from missing the bus just about every day in my junior high years. It was Angela.

By then, it had been a few years since Theresa and Marianne were there to graciously hold up the bus for my tardy self. They were off to bigger and better things, namely high school, with all of its different modes of transportation. So when Angela started school with me at Holy Rosary, which taught students K-8 across two buildings, she was like a lifesaver.

A very, very loud lifesaver.

In those instances, she reverted right back to her original preschool self, much to my benefit. Standing outside, she'd wait while I scrambled to get my stuff together, forcing the bus driver to wait for her and therefore for me as well. Even in the winter time, she could be found right outside the door, ready to yell when she saw the bus make its stop at Sunset Court about 200 yards down the road.

As soon as that happened, she'd start shouting. "Bus! The bus is coming! Come on, Michael! The bus is coming!"

All hell would instantly break loose in the kitchen.

"Come on!" my poor, exasperated mother would demand. "I am not driving you to school if you miss the bus. Let's go!"

I'd be running around like mad.

She'd shift gears.

"I don't know why you don't just get up five minutes earlier so we don't have to go through this every morning!" Whether intentionally or not, Mom would put special emphasis on those last two words.

Yet thanks to me, we did. Every morning. It was predictable routine. The bus would pull up as I shoved the last bit of breakfast in my mouth. Angela would be screaming that the bus had arrived, the bus driver would be laying on the horn, and Mom would be pushing me out the door to catch it before it left.

Looking back, I now realize that if I hadn't had Marianne and Theresa holding up the bus for me in those earlier years and then Angela doing the same after that, I probably never would have made it to high school.

The Family Bridge

It's hard to see Angela as just the youngest in the family. In fact, I'd argue that it's downright impossible. She's a bridge between the third and fourth generations of Marinis I've known.

Angela has an amazing ability to relate to children, and all my nieces and nephews absolutely love her. At family functions she'll hold court with them, and they'll hang on her every word, following her instruction to the letter.

She is an outright celebrity in their eyes… a very big deal.

Then again, she always is.

Angela's Angel

It was August 11, 2013, and a big event was waiting to happen. As such, I was alternately gazing up at the sky and answering messages on my phone.

In the family, when a big event is about to happen, a chain of events typically occurs, including lots of calls and a fully employed "text chain" – typically started by Kate – to pass along tons of updates. This time being what it was, there was no shortage of such.

We were waiting on news about Angela. She'd been in labor for 24 hours already, and everyone had their hand on the pulse of what little Angie was dealing with.

On that particular summer night, there happened to be a lightning storm. Every 15 or 20 seconds, the sky would just illuminate like God was turning the light on and off up in Heaven. I watched in utter amazement like I was watching fireworks on the Fourth of July. It was an awe-inspiring distraction while I waited, though it also served to remind me of another awe-inspiring day 30 years before.

That was when Mom and Pop brought Angela home from the hospital. I could feel that seven-year-old kid inside me all over again waiting to meet my seventh sister on the seventh day of the seventh month. I wanted to meet this new addition to the family already, with anticipation building up inside me every moment that passed.

A new little miracle was on its way.

Joy to the World

My phone showed it was 11:11 p.m., and I was just about to make a wish because of it. But that's when my ringer went off in perfect timing.

The name that came up was "Angel." So of course I picked up immediately.

On the other side of the phone was my little sister sounding exhausted and awe-struck and utterly in love.

"I'm a mommy now, Michael!" she exclaimed. "I'm a mommy now!"

It was only fitting that the seventh girl and 13th member of the family would have her own little girl who weighed in at seven pounds, 13 ounces.

I think Carl Sandburg summed it up best when he said, "A baby is God's opinion that life should go on." Each one brings its own

SEVEN

bundle of joy to share with the world – just like my family's "little angel" and all the angels still to come.

CHAPTER 11
Lap Three

Live so the priest won't have to lie at your funeral.

Sitting in the hospital with Pop that night before Christmas, I decided I wasn't going back to my townhome or my job teaching at a small college in North Carolina after the holidays. I knew in my heart that I wanted to be there for Pop and help him get back on his feet.

Of course, I did have to make another drive to take care of certain things first, such as packing more than a mere week's worth of clothes and locking up my place. Plus, I had to inform my employer about the situation.

When I told the college dean I was taking a leave of absence, I was honest and to the point. "I have family business to attend to right now. My father needs me home for a while to help with it."

She didn't question me. My job, she assured, would be waiting for me when I was finished.

And so, just like that, I moved back up north into my parents' house so I could be there to help Pop start his comeback.

SEVEN

A Dark Comedy

Deciding to push the pause button on the rat-race life I'd been running for over a decade was an interesting experience in so many ways. Like my father, I was getting back to the basics; but in my case, it ran the risk of feeling somewhat ridiculous since I was much too old to be living with my parents.

There I was, back in my old room that had long since been turned into a storage closet for all my nieces' and nephews' toys. It still held my old bed and other such pieces of furniture, but beyond that, the specific space I'd lived in during my stay at 2121 was a far cry from the one I was standing in at that moment. All my posters and plaques had been replaced with Disney posters, stuffed animals and picture frames full of memories of the next generation.

As I stared at a poster of Mickey Mouse, the reality of the situation sunk in and how this newest phase of my life felt like a dark comedy.

At first, I'll admit I had a short-lived pity party for myself, wondering whether I was breaking a record for being the oldest person to move back in with his parents. In basketball, it might be the equivalent to having the record for most time on the bench.

I'm happy to say that I wasn't allowed to dwell on that line of thinking for very long though. It was about then that I noticed the only piece of paraphernalia to survive my absence: a quote I'd put above my bed. As I unpacked my bags and put away my clothes in the wooden Amish-made dresser, I stopped and sat down on my bed to look at it.

"It's a Vision Quest"

Displayed in black marker on a white piece of cardboard, Pop's handwriting clearly highlighted one of his all-time favorite quotes, "If this isn't Heaven, it's at least in the same zip code." Right underneath was a yellow Post-It note he'd written for me a few days before the Pneumonia Race.

"Michael, it's a vision quest."

I'd kept that Post-It note ever since to remind me of that time and that night. And all these years later, it proved to have the same power it did before.

The pity party stopped as I recognized – I just knew – that it was my turn to be the coach. Life had come full circle. A son now had the opportunity to help his father out just as his father had so consistently helped him.

It was a moment of truth.

I may have been in my 30s, unmarried and childless, and taking a leave from work to move back in with my parents. But I knew I was right where I needed to be.

On paper, yes, I was looking like a loser. That hadn't changed. Yet thanks to Pop's quote, I didn't care how that paper looked. I didn't care what my life might appear like to an outsider judging me on a "checklist of successes."

In my heart, I once again knew just as strongly as I had in that hospital room that I wanted to be cheering for Pop. Just like he'd done his whole life for me.

I was going to be there urging him on down the backstretch when he was most tired. It was my turn to encourage him to "hit light and float" when the wind was in his face and the odds were stacked against him.

When I found my old dusty running shoes I'd set aside years ago in a basket in the bedroom closet, I thought back on all the miles they'd put in and the even more impressive ones they were coming out of retirement for.

Now they were meant to become walking shoes, a type of sneaker Pop always referred to as his "running shoes" even though he hadn't run in two decades. He stopped racing because of his bad knees. Plus, he was busy raising 11 children, of course.

My running days were behind me too, but the two of us were just about to get started on another goal-minded adventure that would simply be remembered as, "The Comeback." It was clear when we talked that Pop was ready to step in the ring to take another swing.

SEVEN

It was also clear he was going for a win.

Follow the Leader

When Pop first got home from the hospital, Mom worked both the day and night shifts caring for him. And, for the most part, he listened to everything she said.

"Let's go, Dante," she would say as she got his running shoes ready for him. "You're not going to get any better just sitting around on your rocker. It's time to move."

Pop would laugh when she pushed him like that because she sounded so much like him.

Just like when we were kids, Mom never took a break. She just ran her own race, side by side with Pop.

One day after he and I had taken one of our own strolls – always in the afternoon – he told me, "I'm not sure where I'd be without your mother. She's the iron fist behind the velvet glove in our family. She really is a saint."

I could tell he meant every word of it.

"I just follow her lead."

One for the Books

As adults, it was understood in our house that races should be brought up predominantly for laughs. As Pop would sometimes say after a big win, "Act like you've been there before. Run with grace and win with humility. The sound travels twice as far when someone else toots your horn. And a true champion is humble whether they win or lose."

With that philosophy, it's no wonder Pop came up with largely single-phrase titles to describe the most memorable of our track events throughout the years. The Pneumonia Race. The M-O-M Finish. The Fix. Kate's Great Kick. Denise's Double. Denise's Triple. Jimmy's Kick at Killians. The Wig Race. The Gold at Penn Relays. Angela's National Record Attempt.

LAP THREE

Admittedly, there were some longer ones in there too, like The Time Denise Won Gold on the Streets of Disney; Theresa at Carpenter her Freshman Year; and When Denise, Linda, Kate and Patti Ran the 4x100 Meter Relay With Three Pairs of Shoes. Also worth mentioning would be When Daddy Beat Guido – my mom's only ex-boyfriend – in the Masters' Mile… even though he was out of shape and wearing the t-shirt he wore to work and his black dress socks pulled up to his knees.

Whatever race it was, if it came complete with "You can't make this stuff up" or "that's one for the books," you knew it would go down in the family archives.

All the classic races had a title but, again, most of the time we didn't talk about them unless we were joking around with each other. Besides, not all the classics were wins. It was more about the story behind the race.

What it came down to was that Pop was too humble to talk about them after they were over. He liked the excitement and all that good stuff, but talking about it too much after the fact felt like bragging to him. So when he'd recall any of them, he'd much rather just say the title and move on, knowing that no more words had to be spoken.

We didn't need to talk about them because we'd shared the experience, and that was what it was all about: being together for those seized moments.

Second Chances

One of my pop's – many – favorite quotes was posted on his bathroom mirror. This one reads, "It's not about how many times you go down in life. It's how many times you get up that really counts."

He saw it every day, and he lived by that motto during his comeback.

For the first few weeks after he got home from the hospital, he couldn't walk very far, so we often just sat on his favorite Amish bench out on the front porch and talked. One day, when he was feeling especially weak and couldn't make it across the driveway without a break, he simply stopped. Without a word, he turned around, went over to that Amish bench and sat down.

"God has been great to me," he acknowledged. "He's given me a second chance to finish on my terms. I know this is the bell lap, and I'm going for it."

The way he said it, it didn't matter that he was resting as he did.

"Give me the big seven, and nothing can stop me from my finishing kick!" he added. "I want to make God proud of the way I finish this race of life."

Sure enough, for the next several weeks, I watched him rise from the canvas of life like a boxer in a title fight. After getting knocked down and seemingly out, he stood back up at the count of nine to save his life. Or, as he saw it, his life was saved.

One way or the other, he truly did approach each day like a fighter in training for the heavyweight title of the world.

"I've run hundreds of races, but all that was just preparing me for the big race: this race we call life," he told me one day. "I've been training all my life for this time I'm in right now."

Again, this was in the beginning of his recovery, a fact that didn't faze him.

"Sure," he admitted, "I can barely make it 100 yards without feeling winded. But I'll slowly work my way up and get back on track. God is always preparing us, whether we know it or not."

Then he smiled big. "At least in my case, well, I know it!"

Monster Kick

Most days during his recovery, whenever he wasn't walking, he would take up his normal residence on his rocking chair on the porch. Mom had her own rocking chair right next to his, and then there were two couches on either side of them so that the sitting area was in a sort of semi-circle, with my parents at the center.

It was the closest my family would ever get to having thrones.

LAP THREE

Out there, as everywhere else with Pop, things made the most sense to him when he was comparing it to running. So naturally, he spent a lot of his recovery days doing just that.

"I run my race hard, and I just hope I don't run out of gas before the finish line God has set for me," he told me one of those nights. "I'll keep running hard until he pulls me out, but I just hope I have enough left at the end for a monster kick."

He gave a little smile. "When I was in my racing days, I loved sprinting hard at the end when everyone else was dead-tired and out of gas. I'd just hit light and float when I was most tired. The end is when it comes down to heart, and that just so happened to be my favorite part."

How Sweet the Sound

After dinner during those early days, Pop would go out on the porch and just sit with the TV set on ESPN. One night, he called me out to watch the Milrose Games, the famous indoor track meet they have every February at Madison Square Garden. They were getting ready to run the Wanamaker Mile, and he wanted me to come watch it with him.

As we watched the race, he mentioned something about writing a book. It wasn't the first time he had, but he said he'd really been thinking about it a lot lately. That it was one of the things he thought about most when he was really down in the hospital.

"Maybe I could do something nice and write a book for God," he pondered out loud. "He doesn't get the credit He deserves for all the hard work He does down here on earth. Just like it says in 'Amazing Grace,' He 'saved a wretch like me.' I figure I could at least pay Him back by writing a nice little book."

It sounded like a great idea to me.

"Now that I have the time, maybe I can really do it," he went on "Something to let people know He's still hard at work. Something that could inspire people." Pop shook his head in thought. "I've always said, 'Someday, I'm going to write a book.' Well, maybe this is my someday."

He already had a title for it too: *God, Please Don't Move the Finish Line*. When I asked him what it meant, his reply was one that stands out in my mind even now.

"No one wants to die before they cross the tape, regardless of which place they finish. You may be in dead-last the whole race, but if you finish strong, you finish the way we're all meant to finish. You finish like a champion."

He looked out into the horizon. "I just hope I have enough to get to that point."

Not through yet, he reminded me of the week before when he'd told his grandchildren the story of one of his own races – and why he'd told it. "It wasn't about the race. It was about being a champion in my father's eyes."

Grace and Humility

After all our racing days ended, there were still bigger mountains to climb. Pop rarely looked back at the inclines he'd already conquered – not when he had his focus on the peaks still ahead of him.

Of course, he had already done great things. But for him, it was all about how strong he could finish.

It was a cold afternoon during one of our walks when he got rolling once again on comparing life to races. Mom hadn't wanted him to go out that particular day when the weather was so bad. There was a little bit of snow on the ground, and it was already getting close to sunset. Yet against his coaches' advice, he told me to put on my "running shoes."

He still wanted to get in his second walk of the day.

"I know your mother wants me to take it easy, but I feel like walking. Plus, this is the kind of weather that toughens me up," he said as he laced up his shoes.

Mom, meanwhile, was in the kitchen muttering about how crazy he was to go out in the cold for another walk.

LAP THREE

She'd already asked him, "Can't it wait until tomorrow, Dante? You already did enough exercise for the day. Just take it easy tonight." But he told her it was fine and that we'd only be doing a couple Small Scott laps.

In response, she said something in the kitchen that sounded like grudging acceptance. So off we went. As we were heading to the door, he whispered to me to hurry before she changed her mind.

He was bundled up in his usual gear with his gray sweatpants on, gray hooded Champion sweatshirt and a small bath towel wrapped around his neck so that he looked like an old prize fighter coming out of retirement for one last fight. And he most definitely had the eye of the tiger as he opened the door with purpose.

If an outsider was watching, they would have thought he was late for the most important meeting in the world. My pop was on a mission, and it showed on his face.

Going the Distance

As we began our walk, he told me that he actually wanted to try for three Large Scott Laps – even though he'd told Mom it would just be a quick walk. And as we were halfway into our first, he started up with one of his running analogies.

In life, he said, it wasn't necessarily about how you started but more about how you finished. The true measure of a great life was how well you ran even after losing some laps along the way.

"Just keep running your best no matter where you are in the race," Pop told me as the wind blew in our faces. "That's what God wants from all of us. He wants us to run our best no matter what."

I nodded my head in agreement while actively working to keep my teeth from chattering.

"Take the two-mile, for example." He wiped at his eyes. "That was my favorite race to run. Just a simple eight-lap race, but it's not about the eight laps. It's about what you do in those eight laps that matters."

SEVEN

The cold bit into our hands and faces.

"In some races, you may be in dead-last the first couple laps." Pop had to stop talking for a minute to catch his breath. "No one cares who leads the first few laps of an eight-lap race. No one cares who wins the first mile when there is still another to run."

Despite the elements and my concern for him, I had to smile as he continued.

"Life is all about the long run. It's really about going the distance. Why do you think most people prefer *Rocky I* more than any of the other *Rocky* movies? It's all about an underdog going the distance, and that's God's favorite kind of story. People love the underdog."

Not quite done with the analogy, he shook his head. "In a way, God is an underdog these days. But I think He's coming back right along with me."

All the Classics

The wind was starting to kick up, and the sun was slowly fading behind the tall pine trees that surrounded the field. Our shoes were wet and we were both cold, but Pop said he wanted to go for one more lap.

I did try telling him it might be a good idea to head inside before it got any worse. But he just adjusted the towel around his neck, fixed his hood, and insisted on doing one more anyway "for good luck."

Headed straight into a headwind, he picked right back up where he'd cut himself off. "After seven laps, you hear the heavenly sound of the ringing bell – the Bell Lap. It lets everyone in the race know where they are, and it lets them know it's gut-check time.

"If you're winning, you know the pack is coming for you. If the leader is in front of you, then you have to go after him because time is running out. No pun intended."

With that, he gave a light laugh.

"I hear what you're saying, Pop," I encouraged him.

He smiled, knowing that I really did.

"I know I use running analogies about life a lot, but I think that, with God – no matter how tired you may be – it can feel like you're flying down the backstretch. He helps us hit light when we're tired and weak. Every runner knows the feeling I'm talking about."

I thought about my own races, and yes, that sounded exactly right.

Somebody up There Likes Me

He closed his eyes for several seconds. "Back in the hospital, after your sisters came to visit, I could hear that cheer in my ear – 'Hit light. Just hit light!' – whenever I closed my eyes and listened closely with obedience. It was like someone cheering for me not to just finish the race, but to actually win it."

Pop lit up when he said that last part, then went right back to serious again. "You know how my first doctor wanted to cut me open right away? Good thing your sisters were able to stop him. That doctor was not focused."

In my mind, that wasn't entirely accurate. To me, he had been focused, just on himself. I held that opinion back, however. There didn't seem to be any real point in expressing it.

"Without your sisters, that hospital would have been my finish line." Yet there he was, putting one earthbound foot in front of the other. "Your sisters are the reason I can finish the race like a champion still. They had faith and hope. They showed patience in stopping that doctor. I mean, he was ready to cut me open 10 minutes after he met me! The timing was right for him, but it was not right for me."

He shook his head humbly. "What would I be without someone up there looking after me, whether it's God or His angels?"

Another smile then. "I guess someone up in Heaven likes me enough to give me another lap around the track of life. Maybe two laps if I train right and listen to my coaches!"

I was sure that Mom would have something to say about that if she could.

SEVEN

"Well, I don't want to press my luck," he stated, even though Mom would say he already was by walking so long. "If it's the Lord's will that this is my last lap, then let His will be done! He knows the last lap is when I run best anyway."

Plant a Dream and Watch It Grow

That hardly meant he was done walking quite yet, only that there was a moment of silence while what he'd said sunk in for both of us. Just the sound of our footsteps and rustling jackets and the wind all around us.

He nodded as if at an internal conclusion. "Before I met your mother, I wanted to be the best student, the best baseball player, the best son, the best runner and the best friend I could be. It was simple in my head."

I let him talk, taking it all in.

"I didn't want to be in the middle of the pack and be happy about it. I wanted to have a chance to win every race I entered." He gave a little snort of humor. "Of course, I didn't win a lot of them. But the ones that really mattered to me – the big ones – I did."

A new blast of chilly air came at us, but it didn't stop Dad.

"It was simple to me back then. To be a better runner, I just needed to train hard and do all the little things right like getting enough sleep, eating right, getting in all my workouts. That sort of stuff."

The wind kept blowing, not that Pop seemed to care.

"I've learned a few things since then though. Winning is great, but the only thing that really matters is that you gave it everything you had. If you know in your heart that you did the best you could do, no matter what you're doing, then that's when you've really won." There was a strong note of determination in his voice now. "So that's precisely what I'm going to do."

He stopped walking and looked up at one of the huge pine trees around us. "You know, Nu-Nu and I planted this tree."

LAP THREE

I actually hadn't known that before. It made me wonder how many times I'd passed it without appreciating that my grandfather had a hand in its placement.

"It was just a little tree the day we put its roots in. I remember he dug the hole, and I grabbed the little three-foot sapling and put it into its future home."

Perhaps remembering too, the branches around us rustled against each other.

"We planted 20 in one day, and look at them now. They must be 30 feet tall. Imagine all the things they've seen through the years and how much more they'll witness going forward."

The Bell Lap

As we walked, the sun was starting to slowly set, something Pop also pointed out. "See, they're doing the best they can even now. Look at that sunset. Without those trees here, it would only be half as nice."

The thing was, Pop usually didn't talk this way – despite his list of favorite quotes. He was being much more reflective than I'd ever seen him, almost like a light bulb had gone off in his head and he had to share what he was thinking.

"It's funny how life works. First we walk, then we run and, if we're lucky enough, then we walk again. It's the circle of life I suppose, but we can too easily forget which step we're at and where we're supposed to be."

No matter if it's freezing cold outside, I laughed to myself. If Pop wanted to keep talking, I would continue walking.

"The good Lord has given me a second chance to be the best person I can be. That's something I may have needed a little tap on the back about. It was His way of saying, 'Good job, but now let's see what you can really do, Dante. Show me that kick.'"

He chuckled at that. "Seeing your sisters at the hospital that day made me remember something I never should have forgotten. But I got too focused on work that I suppose I put it on a back shelf.

SEVEN

Sometimes, it's really hard to slow down and appreciate what you got – even if that's exactly what you need.

"Hell, you saw what happened during the Christmas business this year. I almost ran myself into the ground."

Pop went on to admit how he'd forgotten the fundamentals. He hadn't stuck to the basics, like the seven certain gifts he found himself surrounded by on Christmas morning.

Witnessing Greatness

Each morning, Pop and Mom would go for a small walk. That was their time, and I didn't interrupt it.

It was his afternoon walks that I was in charge of; that's when we'd make our way around the field. Being that it was winter, the sun would often be well on its way down while we were walking, and that was certainly the setting – complete with those tall pine trees – the next time he opened up.

This time, it was to talk about when he saw one of the greatest racehorses of all time.

The way Pop told it, this was during a business trip to a town where they just so happened to be keeping Secretariat. A friend and colleague traveling with him knew someone at the stable who had agreed to let the two of them in. As such, it seemed like too good an opportunity to pass up.

It was about three or four years after Secretariat had won the Triple Crown, but from my father's perspective, he looked the exact same as when he'd been in his racing prime.

"It was amazing. He was all muscle and walked with the grace of a true champion," Pop reminisced. "Almost like he knew he was the greatest horse ever."

There Secretariat was, strolling around the fields he used to run around while training. Not a care in the world. He'd done his job and knew he'd done it the best he could, shining his brightest when it really mattered. His running days were over now, and he was completely content to walk and take his time.

No fanfare. No screaming fans. No more hard workouts. He looked like he was just getting back to the basics and enjoying every second of it.

"He looked so peaceful and content," Pop remembered. "And in a humble way too."

He stared off into the field. "It's hard to explain. You'd have to have seen it to really know what I mean about the way he carried himself. But there was simply something there."

All Around Town

"That's why people remember greatness. Once you've seen it or heard it, you know you just got a glimpse of what God really thinks we're capable of doing."

Those words stood out so strongly to me in the moment. *"What God really thinks we're capable of doing."* What a concept to fathom.

"Maybe it's in sports," Pop went on. "Maybe it's in music or maybe it's a painting. Heck, I remember watching a guy sweep the floor at the Philadelphia market. And he was great at it."

I could tell he wasn't joking. It made me think of the famous quote by Confucius, "Wherever you go, go with all your heart."

"He looked so graceful and really seemed to be enjoying it. Anytime I saw him, I thought of him as being great at what he did."

That day, my father reminded me how it doesn't matter what we do. It's how we do it. How life is best lived when we take the talents the Lord gives us and use them to the best of our abilities."

Running on Faith

My time at home was coming to an end. I had to return to work. But the day before I left, Pop and I went for one final walk around the field.

He was feeling pretty good that afternoon, so we did two Large Scott Laps and then headed over to the track to walk another mile.

And once again, he was feeling rather chatty.

"I couldn't have done this walk a couple months ago," he admitted. "That's for sure. You've helped me come back, and now I want to finish strong."

According to him, back in college, his coach told him he had the best kick he'd ever seen in 30 years of coaching runners. Coach Steers used to tell Pop he just had a nose for the finish line, and Pop sincerely hoped he was right. Because, today, he wanted to put that kick into gear in a special way and make the Big Man upstairs proud of him.

"I want to please God. It's as simple as that. I want to finish strong for the Coach of all of us. I'm trying to give Him a happy ending because He gave me another chance to finish on my terms."

God had Pop right where he needed to be. He had him running on faith.

Spirit Writers and Underdogs

As we headed back home, Pop gave me a pat on the back. "It was great having you home, Michael! You've helped me more than you'll ever know."

He smiled, but not in a way that detracted from what he said next. "I promise I'll keep up my training like you told me. And maybe I'll start writing that book like I said I would."

It was my turn then. "Thanks for letting me stay here, Pop. You've helped me out just as much as I've helped you. It was nice to get back to the basics for a bit."

It truly was. They say you can't come back home. Clearly though, they were wrong there.

Further inspiration struck me. "As for that book, I can't say I'm much of a writer; but maybe to pay you back, I can help you write it."

Pop cocked his head to the side. "You mean like one of those spirit writers that famous people get to write their books when they can't do it themselves?"

That made me laugh. "I think you mean a 'ghost writer,' and no, it wouldn't be like that."

He moved right on while we approached the house. "I don't want to write a scary book. I want it to inspire people, not frighten them. So no ghost writers in this book. We'll make it a spirit writer instead."

The more he thought about it, the more he was clearly getting into the notion. "I just want it to be simple: something that lets people know God is still working hard up there even in these tough times. Personally, I think He's working harder now than ever. And people should know that!"

How could I not respond to that kind of passion? "We'll do it as a team, and it won't be a scary book. I promise no ghost writers. Just spirit writing. We'll keep it simple and just write an inspirational book straight from our heart."

Despite the seriousness of the undertaking we were talking about, we both had to laugh at the idea of two non-writers talking about writing a whole book. Whether it was ghost writing, spirit writing or just a team effort, we both knew it was going to be a long shot.

But that's why we liked the idea so much.

Opening our big oak front door, Pop looked back at me. "It's probably about a million-to-one shot that you and I could actually publish a book. But for some reason, I like those odds."

I already knew what he was going to say, but there was no way I was going to steal the words from him.

"God loves the underdog!"

Saints Don't Do Dishes

When we got inside the house, he sat down on his rocker and started to take off his running shoes. By that point, Mom was getting ready to start dinner, which we could see through the kitchen window.

Seeing her like that, in her zone with no idea we'd even come back, Pop got back up to go see her.

"Honey," he called out. "We're home from our walk, and I missed you. Hope you don't have any dinner plans, because we are going out to dinner tonight!"

Mom, who loved going out, lit up like a Christmas tree.

"You're not cooking or cleaning any dishes tonight," Pop explained. "Saints don't do those things after they retire." With that, he looked at me, laughing. "Now that's what every wife wants to hear from her husband when he opens the door."

Laughing as well, Mom took off her apron and gave him a big hug and kiss, then hurried to her room to get changed.

Pop got a good chuckle at how fast she agreed to his offer. But it was obvious he'd meant every word he'd said to her as we both sat down at the table with a glass of water. The way he told me, being the greatest husband he could be was now officially at the top of his to-do list.

It wasn't like he hadn't already known what a wonderful teammate Mom was, but being in the hospital had brought that fact into clear and close focus. And he wanted to remind her about that in no uncertain terms, hence the reason why he yelled at the top of his voice so Mom could hear him in their room.

"Put on your nicest dress, honey! We're going to live it up because you deserve it. How does Café Napoli sound? I know it's your favorite!"

We could both hear her giggle in response.

"You hear that?" He took a sip of his water. "Your mother's laugh is music to my ears."

Then he looked at me with a big smile on his face. "Just doing the best I can at what's number one on my list."

CHAPTER 12
Hitting Light on the Bell Lap

You only live once. But if you do it right, once is enough.

It was a sunny Sunday afternoon, and the date was October 13, my father's birthday. It had been 10 months and 13 days since he was discharged from the hospital, and seven whole months since I'd been home because teaching college took up a lot of my time.

The first thing he said after hugging me was, "I'm almost a year into my comeback!"

He had a light about him as he said it. Like he was feeling good and just going with the flow. Contentment seemed to be oozing out of him.

Unlike with my last visit, I only had one job this time around. And I knew I could handle it. As usual, my sisters took care of all the food and major details, leaving the easy jobs to my brothers and me. Essentially, they'd assign us something we had no chance of screwing up – although we sometimes still managed to do so. Somehow. Someway.

Not this time though. My assignment was to get Pop out of the house for an hour and then bring him in for the big surprise party. So all I did was tell him I'd go along on his birthday walk.

SEVEN

"I hope you've been training," he warned, "because now I can go for an hour."

I assured him I would do my best to keep up.

As we strolled along, we caught up on everything, especially how far he'd come since our last walk in the winter. And we joked and laughed about life, from what the grandkids had been doing to what a great season the Phillies had. Plus, since the Christmas business was right around the corner, we talked a lot about that as well.

He couldn't wait for the business to start up again for another round. It was like he was a baseball player in spring training, and he thought his team had a good chance at going all the way.

A Little Advertising

No matter that the last season had almost killed him. Or maybe it was because of it. Maybe he felt so light approaching the holiday season because he knew what to do – and what not to do this time around.

"This is our year," he declared. "It's going to be our best year yet! I feel it in my bones. Now that the grandkids are getting into it, there's no telling what the business can do."

The conversation then shifted to talk about "all that 'Spacebook stuff" businesses could advertise on. "Can you believe we've been in business for 49 years, and we never really advertised for the Christmas business?"

Truth be told, advertising was something he hated to do. To him, it added to the business by not telling people about it. By letting them find us. It was like some kind of secret he wasn't ready to let out of the bag because he never wanted to substitute quality over quantity.

This was a big deal for him and the source of many fights in the family over the years. My siblings often gave him a hard time for not advertising.

"Why are we wasting our time doing this business if we don't want people to know about it?" they'd demand.

But Pop would stubbornly come back with, "Everyone loves a hidden gem, and that's how we're in this business. We're under the radar – like a club, and every one of our customers is a member."

I had no plans to start any fights. However, since the subject had come up, I decided to put in my own two cents. "Just put an advertisement in the paper this year. It'll cause a lot less drama during the season and be one less headache to deal with. Just look at it that way."

With that, he put his head down and sighed. "Well, I guess you're right. A little advertising won't hurt business too much."

Perfect Timing

Timing is everything in life, sports and relationships. That's something he'd taught me well. I suppose he had that in mind while we made our way down the backstretch.

"What do you say we finish this last lap strong?" he asked. "When we hit the final stretch, we'll kick it."

In all my years, I'd never seen my pop sprint. Sure, I'd seen him jogging when I was a kid. But his racing days were long behind him once I was born, and I never had a chance to really see him run.

As such, I told him I didn't think it was a good idea for him to be running. But he insisted it was how he wanted to finish his 77th year on earth. And I gave in.

How do you argue with your father on his birthday?

As we rounded the final turn to head for the homestretch, he gave me a look and took off running – well, actually fast jogging. He was moving with everything he had in him, and that put him slightly above a trotting pace.

Here's the thing though... on his face, he looked like he was running a sub-4-minute mile, which was awesome to see.

I took off after him for that final dash down the last 100 meters, with me in the first lane and him in the second, "the lane of hope."

That's what Pop used to call it: the lane of hope. It was because, the way he saw it, on the last stretch of the last lap going into that final straightaway, runners could sometimes be going so fast that their momentum took them right out into the second lane.

And that was a good place to be. The second lane always allowed for a clear shot to the finish line – a clear view of what you're going for. One last reminder that you still have a chance.

He ran with sheer determination on his face as we made our way down the homestretch. And crossing the finish line, he threw his hands into the air to yell, "I'm back!"

On the one hand, I was extremely impressed. On the other, I was rather concerned at how heavily he was breathing now.

He, however, was concerned about something else. "Don't tell anyone about this. I want to surprise everyone else on Christmas Eve, but I wanted to show you first."

I promised I wouldn't.

Assured at my pledge, his next words seemed to completely switch topic. "I want to thank you for playing the piano for me that day. You remember when we went down to the hospital lobby and I was in my wheelchair?"

I nodded. "Of course I remember, Pop. It was the start of your comeback. I'm just glad I was there to see it."

Still a little winded, he put his hands on top of his head and took some deep breaths, then started to walk again just like he'd taught us to do. Standing still makes muscles tight.

"You know, it was no coincidence I realized all that stuff after your sisters came to visit me. Almost felt like God was handing me the keys to life while giving me a second chance to live it. The greatest gifts I could ever ask for, and what a day to receive them."

He smiled. "God really has such perfect timing."

One for Good Luck

I could tell he was a little tired now, so I suggested we cool down and then head on home.

He looked at his watch. "You're probably right. It's 3:33, and your mother told me to be home no later than four. She said we may have a little get-together for my birthday, but I think everyone's pretty busy. So it may only be a little group."

He was completely at peace, and I could see a certain joy in him too. It was a small but distinct twinkle in his eyes, though not at the inaccuracy of his birthday-gathering assessment. He was just full of faith and hope, with love pouring out of him as well.

Plus, he was still pleased as punch that he'd run so fast. Not that he was going to give himself all the credit for that. Hardly.

"Everyone helped me get to this point," he declared. "Your mom, your sisters, your brothers, you, all the grandchildren: My entire team brought me back and got me on this track. Especially my two coaches who guided me every step of the way, each and every day."

It almost sounded like he was reciting a poem when he said it, but it was just his thoughts that happened to rhyme.

Reborn

Finally fully catching his breath, he asked me if I wanted to walk one more lap and then head back to the house, which sounded perfect for the party's plan.

As we headed down the backstretch that final time, he went back to expounding on his journey, talking about how he hadn't thought he'd ever run again. But then something clicked inside of him while he was walking.

"I mean, it's been years since I ran," he acknowledged, "but one day, for some reason, my body told me to pick up the pace."

It had been a few months ago while he was out for one of his afternoon walks. Mom was still walking with him in the mornings, and the grandkids might go with him if they were visiting. But for the most part, his "afternoon walks" were done alone, so he started to turn those solitary walks into solitary jogs.

"At first, I couldn't go 50 yards without stopping. Kind of sad for once being a runner," he said. "But I just stuck with it every day; and I knew when I hit a mile, I was back. I didn't tell anyone because I knew they'd stop me, saying it was too dangerous."

That, they definitely would have, I agreed in my head.

"Yet my body was telling me to run. With each step, I felt like I was gaining strength." He grinned. "If my life was a musical score, the orchestra would have started up the montage the day I started running again. I felt reborn and new, inside and out."

"Maybe that's how old Secretariat felt that day I saw him," he mused. "Because, at one point, while we were watching him walk around, he started into a beautiful gallop. Almost like he was saying to all his spectators, 'Don't worry about me. I still have it.'"

I've Been to a Lot of Parties...

With the house right ahead of us now on our walk back, I made sure to sound casual when I asked him what time it was, hearing Linda's voice in my head as I did. Four o'clock sharp. Those were my instructions.

So when he told me it was 3:58, it was downright joyful music to my ears. Thank God I hadn't screwed up my one and only job of the day.

Walking up the stone stairs he'd built with his own hands almost a half-century before, Pop was pretty pleased too. "Well, we made it on time. Life is all about timing, and I go off what time your mother tells me to be home to eat."

We both laughed, knowing how the only time he was ever early for anything was when it came to eating. My particular laugh may or may not have also held a twinge of delight that he really had no idea about the surprise party he was walking into. I could tell that much without a shadow of a doubt, and that was a big deal.

In my family, it isn't easy for secrets to stay secrets for long. So the fact that this one hadn't popped out of the bag was a miracle in and of itself.

Then again, there were a few factors on our side. We'd never thrown a surprise party for him in the past, and he was only turning 78 – not a milestone like 80. So why should he think we'd make a big deal out of it?

The thing was though that Pop loved birthdays. After every birthday party, he'd proclaim one of his famous lines, this one all his… "I've been to a lot of parties, but this one has been the best!"

We'd heard it so often now that it was a running family joke. Someone would start out the phrase, "I've been to a lot of parties, but…" and then trail off, knowing everyone would understand how to finish it.

On this particular birthday afternoon, Pop opened up the big oak front door at 3:59 – with one minute to spare – officially starting a party that most certainly lived up to his famous quote.

When all was said and done, it truly was the best party he'd ever been to.

LUCKY CHAPTER 13
In the Lane of Hope

If this isn't Heaven, it's at least in the same zip code.

I woke to a knocking at my door on Christmas Eve morning.
"Michael, are you ready to go?"
It was Pop, and I sprung out of bed to put my work clothes on for the final day of business. The clock read 7:13 a.m.
"I'm ready, Pop!" I called out while grabbing up my boots.
With that, I heard him walk to the front door and open it, confident I was on my way.
The sun was slowly rising as I took my first step outside. Pop was already out in the garage, sweeping the floor when I walked up the driveway, and I knew he was in a good mood the second I saw him. As I walked toward him, he smiled especially bright.
"We only have 20 trees left," he exclaimed. "Maybe we can sell out this year!"
Selling out was a big deal to him, and it wasn't entirely because of the extra income. It also meant we'd found a home for every tree that was cut.
"It's a sin to see a tree without a home on Christmas morning," he would declare with a shake of his head. "It just isn't right for a tree to get this far and not get to spread its joy during the holiday

season."

Reaching for a broom, I helped him clean up the floors that had held us up for yet another year. This time around was extra special for two reasons, one being that it was our 50th year: the business's golden anniversary. And two, we almost didn't get to celebrate it with Pop.

Last year, when he was fighting for his life, could have gone so much differently.

Everyone in the family, obviously, remembered that latter detail. But as for the former, who knew. None of my siblings kept track of how long we'd been operating. That was Pop's thing. At the end of each year, he would say the number, and that would be it.

This time around, he said it with such pride that he began to tear up. "How do you like this one for God's story? This is the 50th year of the business, which means God kept me in the race to get the gold. Boy, oh boy, He sure is good. He's always writing the perfect story for each of us."

How could I disagree with that sentiment when he was living proof of it standing right there in front of me?

"That's the beauty of it all," he expounded. "He talks to all of us differently. That's why it doesn't matter your religion, race or creed. We just need to see God's story for each of us."

He grinned. "I can see my story, and the cover of the book is solid gold. Because I won God's race – for Him. He believed in me every step I took, and His grace got me through the difficult parts of the journey."

The steps where he stumbled, Pop explained, only taught him a lesson that ended up getting him one more step toward the finish line. One step closer to Him.

Maybe it was a vision quest after all, he mused. Running down that golden street of Heaven to the waiting arms of God above.

Questions and Answers

It had become a tradition for Pop and me to work on Christmas Eve while the rest of the family ran around getting last-minute gifts, preparing for the holidays, and making our traditional seven fishes Christmas Eve dinner. But for him and me, we still liked to be in the trenches together.

It was only fitting that we kept the tradition going, especially because we had missed it the previous year.

"You know," he began, "something happened when you were home that really struck me. It had the biggest impact on my entire recovery, and it happened one night while I was really low."

Wracked with pain, Pop admitted that he didn't know why God had even bothered keeping him alive. He figured he'd made a mistake in the hospital thinking that God had a better plan for him. And so, hurt and angry and afraid, he started yelling at God.

It was the first time he'd ever done something like that. "With all the things He'd already blessed me with, there I was yelling at God Almighty." He shook his head. "I was acting like a real jerk. Demanded that He send me a sign to let me know He was actually cheering for me."

When he opened up his Bible in a challenge to see that sign, the first line he read just blew him away. It made him realize he was part of a much bigger story than he could have ever imagined.

"Someday, I'll tell you what it said," he assured. "But for now, it's between me and the Big Guy."

From the look in his eyes, I could tell that whatever he'd read had a profound effect on him. It was clear that God had answered his question immediately.

A Story of Hope

He seemed to be bursting at the seams with excitement as he talked, his hands moving this way and that while he decorated another wreath. Even though there were still 15 to sell, he was making more. It was classic Pop.

The way he saw it was simple. It was better to have stuff than to not have stuff.

No one else in the family understood this as much as I did. It's part of what made Christmas Eve so special for the two of us: the one day of the year we could both shine our brightest – both of us hitting light in the lane of hope at least once a year.

Win-Win

As our self-imposed work day came to a close and we began to clean up, I asked Pop what we were going to do with the three trees we had left. Usually, we would cut them up and make wreaths. But being that it was four o'clock and dinner was going to start at six, we knew that wasn't going to happen.

Yet I could tell he was hesitant to throw them away.

We ultimately decided to drive them across town. We knew a guy in Little Italy who stayed open late on Christmas Eve – an out-of-the-way competitor of ours – and he'd be glad to take them from us for free. He could make a little money, plus he'd find them a home.

This was a win-win situation for Pop. The way he saw it, the trees would find a home and our competition would think we had a bad year because we didn't sell out. "I like when the competition underestimates me," he said as we walked over to his pickup truck.

Even so, I could see he was a bit sad about the outcome as we reached for the first tree. "Well, maybe it wasn't a perfect ending after all," he declared with a small sigh. "But close enough, right?"

The Perfect Tree

Pop's beat-up, red, 1981 Ford pickup was nicknamed "The Tank" because it had proved to be so reliable over the years. It had over 250,000 hard miles on it, and he said it was just getting warmed up. So, naturally, that's what we were loading the trees into when a minivan pulled up into the driveway. It was a lady driving all by herself, and she had a look of utter unhappiness on her face.

At Pop's cue, I walked on over to her, and she rolled down her window.

"Do you have any trees left?" She asked, trying to hold back tears.

"We sure do!" I declared. "Your timing is perfect. We have three really nice ones left that are looking for a home."

With those words, her face cleared up with absolute relief and an actual smile emerged. "I've been driving around for so long. I'm so glad I found you guys because I really wanted a tree this year, but I just haven't made the time to find one until today."

She climbed out of the minivan, and I began to walk her over to the trees that Pop had already stood up against the side of the truck.

"Take your pick!" Pop said with laughter in his voice. "We couldn't find a home for them for some reason, but they're all winners! And I know they're happy to see you."

Standing there looking at them, a single tear slid down her face. "They're a little bigger than what I was looking for," she admitted. "Is there any way you could trim one down for me? I only need it to be about four feet high."

Nobody needed to cue me this time. I grabbed the best-looking one in the group, a Frasier fir, and brought it over to where we kept the saws. It may have started out as a seven-foot tree, but it sure looked stunning once I cut it down to size.

"Now that is the perfect tree!" Pop said as I held it up to show the lady.

She stood silent in agreement, her eyes once again filling with tears, just happy ones this time.

Another Christmas Miracle

"I can't tell you two what this means to me," she said. "I don't mean to be so emotional, but this tree is very special and I didn't think I was going to find one."

She reached into her wallet to take out some money, but Pop told her to put it away.

"This one is on God," he told her. "He wants to let you know He's cheering for you. You just give this tree here a nice place to sleep tonight."

We both figured it would make her Christmas, but it was clearly making Pop's too.

"We're just glad to find it a home," he added. "It was close to being all alone on Christmas, and now it has a true home. It was a million-to-one-shot, and you saved it."

"Are you sure?" she asked.

He didn't hesitate. "This tree has been growing for 10 years and it found its home in the final hour. This is the biggest moment of this little tree's life!"

The lady put her wallet away and began to walk to her car as I followed her with her gift. It was a great way to end the day, I thought. Though, as it turned out, it wasn't entirely over quite yet.

As I was putting the tree in her trunk, she grabbed my arm. "Thank you so much. Really, this means so much more than I can possibly express."

The level of sincerity in her voice took me by surprise. I'd figured before that she was just tired from the searching, but there was something in her voice now that clued me in. This wasn't just about the tree.

She wiped away more tears. "My son passed away two months ago from cancer. He was only 13 years old, but he loved Christmas more than anything."

The pain was written all over her face now. But there was something else there too.

"I used to buy a little tree to put in his room every year, and the last promise I made him was that he would always have a tree next to him when he wakes up on Christmas morning."

She began to cry then but quickly composed herself. "I'm going to his grave right now to put it up. He'll be so excited."

As she spoke, I could see Pop also paying attention to her words while I tried not to cry myself.

"I will never forget this," she told me. "Not ever."

The smile she gave, teary eyes and all, was downright beautiful. "I have a peace I never thought I'd feel again. I can't thank you enough."

As she got in her car, she yelled to Pop, "Thank you, sir! And God bless you and your family this holiday season!"

With that, she drove out of the driveway and up the street.

Pop and I stood and watched her leave, neither one of us saying a word.

When Angels Shine Brightest

Pop slowly turned around and walked to the house in complete silence, our mission to offload our remaining inventory completely forgotten in the face of something so much bigger. We'd just been given proof that God really does like happy endings.

Closing the garage doors and putting away the brooms, I was filled with the sense that the season had ended on the absolute perfect note. It was a feeling that stayed with me as I walked down the path to the little porch, where Pop was taking off his boots.

This was always a process for him considering how much he laced them up every day. Usually, he needed someone to pull them off altogether.

He didn't look up when I walked over. He didn't say a single word. But I saw tears hitting his boots as he tried to take them off.

"Are you alright, Pop? Do you need help?"

He remained silent for another moment. Yet I knew he was crying, which was extremely out of character for him.

"You see, Michael," he finally said, "that's God's way of patting me on the back for a good season. And it's my way of telling Him thank you."

There was so much gratitude and even awe in what he said and how he said it. "It's God's script, and He knows how to finish strong. If I ever write a book, I will end it with a miracle just like that one."

I loved the sound of that.

"It's His way of saying He's still working hard and pulling for the underdog," Pop added, resorting to repetition that I didn't mind. These were the sorts of sentiments that needed to be repeated.

"God's timing is perfect, and what just happened here was a small miracle." He shook his head. "What a way to end."

What a way to end indeed.

Our Father's Story

With that, he put his boots to the side of the bench and took up his running shoes. Meanwhile, we could hear laughter and plenty of other interactive sounds coming from the kitchen. Most of the family had arrived for the traditional Feast of the Seven Fishes, and it showed.

"One year ago today, I was flat on my back," Pop reminisced. "That's when I truly saw how it's not my story. It's God's, and He will tell it the way He sees fit. Our job is simply to follow His script."

After he finished lacing up his running shoes, he stood up. The sun was setting and, from where I was sitting, I could see it slowly lowering behind the trees in Scott's field.

Pop opened the door and began jogging that way, the hop in his step making him almost look like he was skipping.

It certainly was God's script, and my father was following it down to the letter.

His parting words as he headed to the field summed it up perfectly. "We're not just in the same zip code as Heaven, Michael. We're actually in it."

REVELATION
The Finish Line

Those walks and meaningful talks with my pop opened my eyes to my own journey in life. Because I was, in fact, on a journey. We all are in one way or another.

We're all searching to hear our true hearts' song and to understand the meaning of life.

Sometimes, it may be a tragedy that brings us face to face with the answer. Sometimes it's observing or interacting with others who then shed that light. For me, it was a number of elements, those walks and talks included.

But it was also something else. Someone else, actually. Seven of them.

Weeks before I came home to start getting Pop back on his feet, my sisters were already busy on that mission, sharing their gifts on that memorable Christmas morning. The seeds of the spirits sowed in my sisters emerged to blossom in perfect timing.

Just like they'd blossomed so many times before.

Just as they would again in upcoming seasons.

My sisters reawakened my father's outlook on life, and mine as well. They inspired us to let our lights shine as brightly as the good

Lord created us to do. They encouraged us to continue on our journeys with renewed purpose and passion.

This is our story – his, mine and my family's – that I am so blessed to be able to share. The angel in that fated dream 17 years ago was right. The seven spirits I saw at the kitchen table had truly guided the way.

In the beginning, I saw them as my seven sisters. In the end though, they were seven of the most important gifts God gives each of us to fuel us along the way. They were the keys to opening the golden book the angel handed me in that unforgettable dream.

The Light

It wasn't that long ago that Pop randomly asked me, "Whatever happened to that book we talked about writing? The world needs a good story today."

And perhaps God thought it was time to tell His story as well. A story spreading hope, offering love, bestowing peace, encouraging faith, practicing patience, granting grace and transmitting joy. In these current times of tragedy and darkness, those are all great ways to wrap ourselves in the wisdom and love of our Father, who's always there, ready to light the way.

It's far too apparent how much darkness there is around us today. People hate each other. Children suffer. Wars and man-made famines and destruction happen.

Darkness. It seems to be everywhere. Seeing this, some people even believe the world can't take much more and we're truly in the end times.

But that's going to change. It's already changing, in fact. We just need to know where to find that promise and how to hold onto it so we can share it and let the light spread so much further than ourselves.

In these times, we have to remember to stay in the light. That's where God is. That's what God is.

And God wants to move. Like my earthly father, He is ready to run. Like my earthly father, He wants to show His family how He still has a big kick coming.

He is still the Champ.

He still wants to reach us.

He still wants to reach you.

SEVEN

Those outright passionate efforts on His part are geared toward proclaiming one simple message. They're all about His desire to say, "I love you. Please let me show you how much."

THOUGHTS FROM THE HEART

During Pop's comeback, I'd often sit with him in the evenings. As my sisters put it, my job was the nightshift. Mostly, we watched old boxing matches and ESPN. But on occasion, he would shut off the TV and start composing what he deemed his "thoughts from the heart." The setup was quite simple. I would take my own spot while he rocked in his chair, his feet propped up and his eyes closed.

One of the nights he summed it up best when he said, "At this point in my life, I've put it all in God's hands. I tell him that all the time too. In fact, my conversations with God are becoming so frequent that I feel like I'm earning my doctorate in prayer."

Below, I've included those "thoughts from the heart" resulting from all that prayer time.

Half-Full

I have dreamed a lot along the way,
running this race of life day after day.
Dreams float along and slowly pass,

but it's all how you look at the glass.

Sometimes the tide of life is flowing,
and you're in that flow without even knowing.
The cup of life is half-full when you look at it;
just say your prayers and the rest will fit.

Days will come and nights will pass.
In the end, it's all about how you look at the glass

Getting Back in the Race

I slowed down a bit this lap around.
Next lap I will float, I won't even touch the ground.
I was out for a bit, not even in the race;
but this next lap, I will slowly increase my pace.

I'm on the bell lap now and it's time to go.
From here on in, I will not slow.
It's not as important how you start;
rather how you finish and what's in your heart.

Another dream is about to start, and I can't wait.
My father was right when he said it all comes down to fate.
Visions pass before my eyes, so many things to see.
Nothing is ever a surprise when you believe it's meant to be.

Time to get back and return to the basics, I suppose.
I'm stepping back on that track to chase the fate God chose.

Dusting Myself Off

Another day brings another dream,
filling all the gaps I missed in between.
Time to dust myself off and go:
prove to myself what I already know.
This is a comeback that I am mounting,
with passing days that I am not counting

I will try my best and hope it's enough.
If I should fall, I hope the Lord will pick me up.
Dust off the racing shoes; it's time to come back.
Going to toe the line and burn around life's track.
It's been some time, but I have no fear;
for when I listen to my heart, I can hear the angels cheer.

Waiting for That Call

It seems that now the future is clear
My next big move is coming. It's getting near.
This next lap in life, I will make my biggest move.
I will fly down that backstretch, running nice and smooth.

Dreams I see are just up ahead
as visions of hope swirl around my head.
Late in the race is when I really start to groove.
It was when no one expected it that I made my move.

I liked when they counted me out early in a race
because it takes me time to really find God's pace.
Ready to face a giant without an ounce of fear,
my next move is coming. It is very near.

When it is time to go, I will give it my all.
But for now I sit in my rocker and wait for His call.

Small Wonder

Lately dreams have been flooding my mind
of all the hopes and visions I wish to find,
getting back to all that I left behind.
Just going to keep smiling and always be kind.

Trying to weather the storm to get to the shore;
letting my mind open another door.
How it all will end I am not sure.

SEVEN

I will just press on, and I will endure.

Float through the wind, light as air,
Making sure to get things right with delicate care.
Your mother and I, we are quite a pair
Just want to finish without a second to spare.

Running to the light

Just sitting here, staring into space,
hoping to finish strong and win life's race.
Holding on as days seem to fly by,
when I need answers, I point my eyes to the sky.

I just wonder if I am slipping away or is this my comeback;
am I heading into the light or coming out of the black?

Time to Spare

I wonder if I can do it – if I can see it through:
that dream in the distance, the one I always knew.
Fears can sometimes get the best of me.
They can cloud my vision to that vision I see.
Everything around me seems to be passing by so fast.
Trying my best to shake off setbacks of the past.
Sometimes lost in between here and there,
just want to reach that finish line with time to spare.

I Press On

I woke up last night with ideas running around my brain,
so I prayed to the good Lord to help explain.
So many thoughts came at once, so I tried to keep up.
They were flowing like water, so I searched for a cup:
something to help me hold onto all that was coming through.
So many passing faces, changing from old to new.
Hard to keep up with all that I could see;

just trying my best to be the man I wish to be.
Day by day, I am slowly seeing what needs to be done.

Even in these hard times, my faith is not gone.
The last thing I remember was a voice whispering, "Press on."

Late Kicker

On this day, I am very clear.
Some changes in my life are very near.
Just like in a race, I put my head down and go.
It's what the next lap brings that I do not know.

All I have is what is deep inside.
God is my coach and we run stride for stride.
I was never very good in races at the start.
I was better late in the race when it came down to heart.

No Regrets

Inside each day, there is a dream to be found:
messages that may come into your heart without a sound.

I just step back and watch it all unfold:
A story familiar to many, but never told.
Visions in my mind, I am starting to see.
A key to Heaven, it was given to me.
An answer to every question lies deep in our hearts.
Our Creator has made each soul its own work of art.

Make each day one that you will never forget
without a second missed or a single regret.

Heaven Is Here

Heaven is all around
when I gaze at the sky. When I look at the ground.

SEVEN

It makes no difference who you are:
Heaven is all around. It is not very far.
Every child that I see, every day that passes,
I look at it all through the lenses of God's glasses.
Now when I see the world, it is very clear:
I'm not waiting for the gate to open, Heaven is here.

POP'S QUOTES THROUGH THE YEARS

YOU ONLY live once. But if you do it right, once is enough.

EVEN THOUGH the horse is blind, just load the wagon.

I DON'T mind if you throw tomatoes at me. As long as you take them out of the can first.

THERE IS a price to be paid for success. That price MUST be paid in advance.

TOUGH TIMES don't last. Tough people do.

WE'RE NOT where we want to be. We're not where we should be. But we're sure as hell NOT where we used to be.

WHEN YOU see someone doing something you can't do, they just know something you don't know.

THERE ARE three types of people in this world: the type that make things happen, the type that watch things happen… and the type that say, "What the hell just happened?"

LIVE SO the priest won't have to lie at your funeral.

THAT'S WHY people remember greatness. Once you've seen it or heard it, you know you just got a glimpse of what God really thinks we're capable of doing.

ANYBODY CAN be a grandfather, but it takes a special person to be a pop-pop.

IF YOU'RE lucky enough to be Italian, you're lucky enough.

HE BUYS his employees. I raise my own.

IF MORE kids were self-starters, then parents wouldn't have to be cranks.

WHEN WE fail to change, we fail.

IF YOU ever decide to have 11 children, you'd better be ready to work!

LIVE FOR today, dream for tomorrow and learn from yesterday.

YOUR TALENT is God's gift to you. What you do with it is your gift to God.

GOOD. BETTER. Best. I never let it rest. Not until my good is better and my better is best.

CHARACTER IS what you do when no one is looking.

YOU HAVE three names in this world. Your family name, the name your family gives you, and the name you make for yourself.

KEEP YOUR eyes on the fundamentals.

THERE ARE only three things you need to do each day: Laugh, love and learn.

YOU'RE RIGHT where you need to be.

IT'S GOT a chance. – said after he read over a rough draft of this book.

ABOUT THE AUTHOR

Michael J. Marini is a professional pianist (whose favorite time to play is after midnight), an educator, the proud uncle to 27 nieces and nephews, and the proud godfather of three. When it comes to sports, he's all about Philadelphia – a hardcore "four for four for life" fan. And though he's an all-around sports enthusiast, he particularly enjoys boxing and baseball… including their history. You can easily find him reading sports or musical biographies in his downtime, or watching *Columbo* reruns. He and his wife, Wendy, live in Central Pennsylvania with their dog, Gus "the lovebus," an ambassador of goodness wherever he goes.

If you've enjoyed what you read and heard, Michael would love to hear about it. Leave a rating and review on Amazon and/or Goodreads. And please visit **TheSpiritOfSeven.com** to see what he's up to now!

MUSIC TO ACCOMPANY *SEVEN*

Pleiades, the complementary soundtrack to *Seven*, is also available on Spotify, Apple Music, Amazon and iTunes.

Look up "Spirit of Seven" on your choice platform… or visit **SpiritOfSeven.HearNow.com** to experience the musical version of the message you just read.

Made in the USA
Columbia, SC
11 November 2018